need to know?

Speak
French

Collins

First published in 2005 by Collins
an imprint of
HarperCollins Publishers
Westerhill Road, Bishopbriggs
Glasgow G64 2QT

www.collins.co.uk

A catalogue record for this book is available from
the British Library

Editor: Caroline Smart
Text: Harry Campbell
French consultant: Gaëlle Amiot-Cadey
Series design: Mark Thomson
Photographs: Penny Tweedle/Getty Images
Front cover photograph: © Penny Tweedle/
Getty Images

isbn 0 00 719329 7

Typeset by Davidson Pre-Press Graphics Ltd,
Glasgow
Printed in China

Contents

Word Zone

Introduction

Are you one of those people who want to learn French, but have never quite managed? Perhaps, after numerous attempts, you still don't feel on top of the basics. Then *Collins Speak French* is for you. This course is designed for those with some knowledge of French, but who would like to learn more, or be shown that they do indeed know more than they think.

We do this through a series of dialogues. You can listen to the dialogues on CD1, the Dialogue Zone, and then explore the conversations in more depth in the book. The dialogues provide a snapshot of French while the points highlighted in each dialogue reveal how the language works – sometimes in a logical way, but often not!

We pick out of each dialogue the most important vocabulary, and then add a number of extra words to learn, often on a slightly different theme. Then it's your chance to speak French in the short exercises on the following track.

The middle section is the Word Zone which gives you a basic vocabulary, English to French and French to English.

The final section of the book, the Reference Zone (on CD2), gives you the nuts and bolts – numbers, time, nouns, verbs and so on. Each topic has its own track so you can decide what to focus on and there are lots of examples showing how French works.

Before you begin listening to the dialogues, you might like to see how English and French compare in the Points about English and French on pages 8–9. These give a brief summary of the differences (and similarities) between the two languages.

Collins Speak French is a basic introduction to the language. If you want all the detail, we recommend *Collins Easy Learning French Grammar* and *Easy Learning French Dictionary*.

So that you don't have to rely on listening to the CDs to get the pronunciation right, the book features an easy-to-follow pronunciation system. This means the book and CDs can be used independently. For a full explanation of how to use this course, turn to the *How to use* section Dialogue Zone 1.

We hope that this original approach to language learning is one that works for you, and gives you the confidence to go on and speak French. You may even enjoy it!

Points about English

Mary works in a small shop. She sells cheese, fruit and vegetables. She usually gets up early in the morning because the shop opens at 8 o'clock. She lives in the centre of Manchester.

verbs

These are the words that tell you the action of the sentence: **works**, **sells**. In English you use words like I, she or they (pronouns), with the verb to show who is doing the action: I **go**, you **go**, he **goes**, we **go**, etc. When it's not specified who is performing the action, you sometimes find the word 'to' in front of it: to work, to sell, to be. This is known as the 'infinitive'; you could think of it as the starting point for an 'infinite' number of ways that the verb can go.

nouns and articles

Nouns are labels for anything you can give a name to: **market, cheese, house**. A noun doesn't have to be a solid thing; it can be something abstract like **morning**, or it can be the name of something specific like a person or place: **Mary, Manchester** (such nouns, spelt with a capital letter, are called 'proper' nouns). When there is more than one of something, the 'plural' form is used; in English, this most often involves adding an -s (**markets, mornings**) though many words have irregular plurals (**man/men, sheep/sheep**). In English the definite article is **the**, and the indefinite **a** or **some**.

adjectives

Adjectives are words that describe a thing or person, to give extra information about them: a **small** market, a **tall** girl, **young** Mary, the work is **enjoyable**, Manchester is **big**. In English the adjective generally goes in front of the noun, and it's the same whatever the word it describes: **pretty** girl, **pretty** girls, a **slim** girl, a **slim** boy.

adverbs

An adverb is a word that describes a verb or an adjective – how, when or where something is done: Mary gets up **early**, she drives **carefully** and works **quickly**. Often, though not always, English adverbs are made by adding -ly to an adjective: **careful/carefully**; **quick/quickly**. But many of the most common adverbs are irregular: **early, fast, well**. Examples of adverbs applying to adjectives are **very early, incredibly pretty, really good**.

prepositions

Prepositions usually indicate a relationship such as position or time: **in** a small market, **near** the centre of Manchester, **at** 8 o'clock. Sometimes one language uses a preposition where it is not needed in the other, just as you can say either 'I wrote to my mother' or (in American English) 'I wrote my mother'.

Points about French

Mary **travaille dans un petit** magasin. **Elle vend du** fromage, **des fruits et des** légumes. **Elle se lève généralement tôt** le matin **parce que** le magasin **ouvre à 8 heures. Elle habite le** centre **de** Manchester.

verbs

In French there are various endings according to who is 'doing' the action, eg **tu aimes** 'you like', **nous aimons** 'we like', **ils aiment** 'they like', while English usually has just two: 'like/likes'. French verbs generally divide into three sorts, according to whether the infinitive (which is just one word in French) ends in **-er** (**aimer** 'to like, love'), **-ir** (**finir**, 'to finish') or **-re** (**prendre**, 'to take'). Not all verbs are regular, however, and some of the most common ones are unpredictable, just as in English we normally say 'I am', 'you are' and 'he is' rather than 'I be', 'you be' and 'he bes'.

adverbs

In French most adverbs are made by adding **-ment** to the adjective in its feminine form: **rapide/rapidement** 'quickly'. But as in English, many of the most common adverbs are irregular: **tôt** 'early', **vite** 'fast', **bien** 'well'.

adjectives

In French, unlike English, adjectives 'agree' with the noun they are describing – **petit magasin**. If a word is masculine, the adjective stays in the basic form in which you find it in the dictionary, but if the noun is feminine, a feminine ending (most often **-e**) is added – **petite fille**. If the adjective describes several things (the plural), then the ending shows this, usually by adding **-s** or **-es**. And if a group is a mixture of masculine and feminine, masculine takes precedence.

nouns and articles

In French all nouns are either 'masculine' or 'feminine'. These are just terms to describe the way a word behaves: it doesn't necessarily mean that the thing itself is male or female, so don't waste time worrying what makes a cup 'feminine' but the coffee in it 'masculine'. The words **le** and **la** 'the', and **un** and **une** 'a' (known as articles) are the key: **le/un** is for masculine words (**café**, 'coffee'), and **la/une** is for feminine words (**tasse**, 'cup'). To be sure of the 'gender' of a word you will need to look it up in a dictionary or wordlist, though sometimes you can make an educated guess from the ending. Adding an **-s** is also the standard way to make a plural in French. The plural of the indefinite articles (**un/une**) is **des**, meaning 'some' or 'any'. This has to be included, even though in English we might simply say 'fruit', not 'some fruit'.

prepositions

These work much as in English – **dans** 'in, inside', **sur** 'on', etc – except that sometimes it may not be the preposition you'd expect. For example, in French you are not 'on' the train but 'in' it: **dans** le train, not **sur** le train, which would mean on top of it. Likewise, in Manchester is **à** Manchester 'at Manchester' rather than **dans** Manchester 'inside Manchester'.

Pronunciation guide

We've tried to make it as obvious as possible how to pronounce the French in the book, by giving a phonetic transcription (re-spelling) of each word, breaking up words into syllables and using hyphens for clarity.

The consonants are not difficult, and are mostly pronounced as in English; **b f k l m n p s t v x** and **z**.

need to know

h	is always silent
r	should be pronounced at the back of the throat in the well-known French way, although an English-style 'r' will be understood
c	when **c** comes before **e**, **i** or **y** it is pronounced like s; otherwise it is a hard 'k' sound
g	as with **c**, when **g** comes before **e**, **i** or **y** it is 'zh' like 's' in pleasure, not hard 'g'
ç	is pronounced the same as s
q	is always the 'k' sound in kick, not the 'kw' in quick
ch	is 'sh'
gn	is 'ny', something like the sound of 'ni' in onion
w	is either 'v' or 'w'
ou	in French is something like 'oo' in English
u	in French (as in **une**), which some English speakers have trouble with, is not really so hard: just round your lips as if about to say 'oo' but pronounce 'ee'. We use the symbol _oo_ in the pronunciation guide for this sound.
o	there are two sounds in French; one is a little like the 'o' in English hope (but more pure, as in Scottish pronunciation), while the other is more like hop. We've represented the first by _oh_ and the second by _o_ in the transcriptions.

The transcription _uh_ covers three similar sounds: the rounded vowels of both **peu** and **peur**, and the nondescript sound (similar to the unstressed syllables of English ago or sofa) found in **je** _zhuh_ or **se** _suh_ and the first syllables of French **demain** _duh-mañ_ and **retard** _ruh-tar_. Look out for the following letter combinations: **au** and **eau** are _oh_; **oi** is _wa_; **ui** is something like _wee_.

There are various 'nasalised' vowels in French, meaning that they are pronounced partly through the nose. When you see a _ñ_ in the transcription you should nasalise the vowel before it and not pronounce an 'n'. For example _añ_ represents the sound in the French words **main** _mañ_ or **fin** _fañ_ or **rien** _ry-añ_, rather than that of **Anne** _an_. The others are _uñ_ (as in **brun**, _bruñ_), and _oñ_, which we use to cover the similar sounds of **dans** _doñ_, **en** _oñ_ and **blanc** _bloñ_ as well as **mon** _moñ_, **on** _oñ_ and **blond** _bloñ_.

Pronunciation tips

> If a masculine noun or adjective ends in a vowel, its pronunciation does not change when an -e is added to make the feminine. For example, **ami** and **amie** *a-mee* 'male/female friend' are both pronounced the same, as are **joli** and **jolie** *zho-lee*.

> If a masculine noun or adjective ends with a consonant that is not pronounced, for example, -d, -s, -r or -t, you do pronounce that consonant when an -e is added in the feminine. For example, in **étudiant** *ay-too̲d-yoñ* '(male) student', you cannot hear the **t**; in **étudiante** *ay-too̲d-yoñt* '(female) student', the **t** is pronounced.

> When **les** *lay* is used in front of a word that starts with a consonant, you do not pronounce the **s**: **les chiens** *lay shyañ* 'the dogs'. But you do pronounce it when **les** is followed by a word that starts with a vowel, and most words starting with **h**. It sounds like the 'z' in the English word zip: **les amis** *layz a-mee* 'the friends', **les hôtels** *layz o-tel* 'the hotels'. This is known as 'liaison'. The same thing happens with the indefinite article **des** *day*: **des amis** *dayz a-mee* 'friends', **des hôtels** *dayz o-tel* 'hotels'.

> Adding an -s (as opposed to -es) or -x to the end of a noun or adjective does not change the way the word is pronounced. For example, **professeur** and **professeurs** *pro-fe-suhr*, and **chapeau** and **chapeaux** *sha-poh*, sound just the same, as do **noir** and **noirs** *nwar* and **nouveau** and **nouveaux** *noo-voh*.

> When the -s or -x ending comes before a word starting with a vowel or most words starting with **h**, you do pronounce the **s** or **x** on the end of the adjective. It sounds like 'z': **les anciens élèves** *layz oñss-yañz ay-lev* 'the former pupils'; **de grands hôtels** *duh groñz o-tel* 'big hotels'.

> Some words, especially masculine nouns and adjectives, such as **bon** *boñ* 'good' or **italien** *ee-tal-yañ* 'Italian', end in a vowel and -n. With these words, you pronounce the vowel 'through your nose' (a 'nasalized' vowel) but do not actually say the **n** – it's just there to show the nasal quality of the vowel. When the consonant is doubled and -e is added in the feminine – **bonne** *bon*, **italienne** *ee-tal-yen* – the vowel becomes a normal one instead of a nasalised vowel and you do pronounce the **n**.

useful websites

> **French Steps, a new BBC online course for beginners**
  http://www.bbc.co.uk/languages/french/lj/
> **A dictionary of French expressions**
  http://french.about.com/library/express/blexdico-a.htm
> **A French audio dictionary**
  http://french.about.com/library/pronunciation/bl-audiodico.htm
> **A searchable French dictionary**
  http://www.wordreference.com/fr/index.htm

Dialogue Zone

The dialogues provide a snapshot of French, while the points highlighted show how the language works. We pick out of each dialogue the most useful vocabulary and then add a number of extra words to learn, often on a slightly different theme. Then it's your chance to speak French in the short exercise on the following track.

How to use *Speak French*

The book comes with two CDs. Purple CD1, the Dialogue Zone, contains the dialogues, vocabulary and practice. Blue CD2, the Reference Zone, contains the nuts and bolts: numbers, days, months, etc. It goes with the final section of the book.

purple CD1 track number

Dialogue Zone

There are 16 dialogues. Each one begins with an even track number: 2 is 'At the tourist office', 4 is 'A chance encounter' and so on. The practice sessions following each conversation begin with an odd number: 3, 5, 7, etc.

Try listening to the dialogues first, without referring to the book, to see how much you understand.

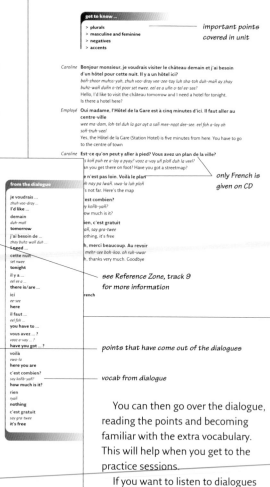

2 At the tourist office

get to know ...
> plurals
> masculine and feminine
> negatives
> accents

important points covered in unit

Caroline Bonjour monsieur, je voudrais visiter le château demain et j'ai besoin d'un hôtel pour cette nuit. Il y a un hôtel ici?
boñ-zhoor muhss-yuh, zhuh voo-dray vee-zee-tay luh sha-toh duh-mañ ay zhay buhz-wañ duñn o-tel poor set nwee. eel ee a uñn o-tel ee-see?
Hello, I'd like to visit the château tomorrow and I need a hotel for tonight. Is there a hotel here?

Employé Oui madame, l'Hôtel de la Gare est à cinq minutes d'ici. Il faut aller au centre-ville
wee ma-dam, loh-tel duh la gar ayt a sañ mee-noot dee-see. eel foh a-lay oh soñ-truh-veel
Yes, the Hôtel de la Gare (Station Hotel) is five minutes from here. You have to go to the centre of town

Caroline Est-ce qu'on peut y aller à pied? Vous avez un plan de la ville?
[...]s koñ puh ee a-lay a pyay? vooz a-vay uñ ploñ duh la veel?
[...]n you get there on foot? Have you got a streetmap?

only French is given on CD

[...]e n'est pas loin. Voilà le plan
[...]h nay pa lwañ. vwa-la luh ploñ
[...]'s not far. Here's the map

[...]est combien?
[...]y koñb-yañ?
[...]ow much is it?

[...]ien, c'est gratuit
[...]añ, say gra-twee
[...]othing, it's free

[...]h, merci beaucoup. Au revoir
[...] mehr-see boh-koo. oh ruh-vwar
[...]h, thanks very much. Goodbye

see Reference Zone, track 9 for more information

More than one
Adding an -s is the standard way to make a plural in French: minute, minutes. Adding the 's' doesn't affect how the word is pronounced. However, you have to remember to make the le and la plural. They both become les (*lay*) which no longer gives any clue to the gender. As in all things, there are exceptions: see the following noun endings -eau, -eu or -al (le bateau-les bateaux, le neveu-les neveux, le cheval-les chevaux). And nouns ending in -s, -x, or -z don't change in the plural. > NOUNS REFZONE 9.

from the dialogue

je voudrais ...
zhuh voo-dray ...
I'd like ...
demain
duh-mañ
tomorrow
j'ai besoin de ...
zhay buhz-wañ duh ...
I need ...
cette nuit
set nwee
tonight
il y a ...
eel ee a ...
there is/are ...
ici
ee-see
here
il faut ...
eel foh ...
you have to ...
vous avez ... ?
vooz a-vay ... ?
have you got ... ?
voilà
vwa-la
here you are
c'est combien?
say koñb-yañ?
how much is it?
rien
ryañ
nothing
c'est gratuit
say gra-twee
it's free

points that have come out of the dialogues

vocab from dialogue

It's a girl!
You'll probably be familiar with the concept of words being masculine (le plan) or feminine (la ville). This is known as 'gender', but it shouldn't be confused with the sex of humans or animals. Although words for things that are male or female in real life usually have the corresponding gender, you can't rely on it. To find out the gender of a word you will need to look it up in a dictionary, though sometimes you can make an educated guess from the ending. > NOUNS REFZONE 9.

What's in the article?
Le, la and les (meaning 'the') are known as definite articles. The indefinite ones meaning 'a' or 'an' or 'some' are un (for masculine nouns), une (for feminine nouns) and des (for both masculine and feminine). The important thing to remember is that des can never be missed out in French, even if there is no corresponding word in English. 'I bought apples and oranges' is much the same as 'I bought some apples and oranges', but in French you have to say j'ai acheté des pommes et des oranges.

You can then go over the dialogue, reading the points and becoming familiar with the extra vocabulary. This will help when you get to the practice sessions.

If you want to listen to dialogues and vocabulary, just stay with the even numbers.

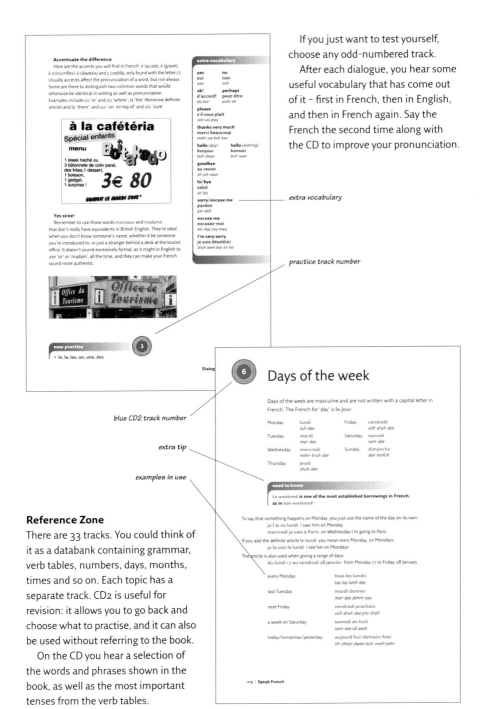

If you just want to test yourself, choose an odd-numbered track.

After each dialogue, you hear some useful vocabulary that has come out of it – first in French, then in English, and then in French again. Say the French the second time along with the CD to improve your pronunciation.

Accentuate the difference
Here are the accents you will find in French: é (acute), è (grave), ê (circumflex), ë (diaresis) and ç (cedilla, only found with the letter c). Usually accents affect the pronunciation of a word, but not always. Some are there to distinguish two common words that would otherwise be identical in writing as well as pronunciation. Examples include ou 'or' and où 'where'; la 'the' (feminine definite article) and là 'there'; and sur 'on, on top of' and sûr 'sure'.

à la cafétéria
Spécial enfants
menu
1 steak haché ou
3 bâtonnets de colin pané,
des frites, 1 dessert,
1 boisson,
1 gadget,
1 surprise !
3€ 80
GRATUIT LE MARDI SOIR*

Yes siree!
Remember to use those words monsieur and madame, that don't really have equivalents in British English. They're ideal when you don't know someone's name, whether it be someone you're introduced to, or just a stranger behind a desk at the tourist office. It doesn't sound excessively formal, as it might in English to use 'sir' or 'madam', all the time, and they can make your French sound more authentic.

extra vocabulary

yes / oui / wee	no / non / noñ
ok! / d'accord! / da-kor!	perhaps / peut-être / puht-etr
please / s'il vous plaît / seel voo play	
thanks very much / merci beaucoup / mehr-see boh-koo	
hello (day) / bonjour / boñ-zhoor	hello (evening) / bonsoir / boñ-swar
goodbye / au revoir / oh ruh-vwar	
hi/bye / salut / sa-loo	
sorry/excuse me / pardon / par-doñ	
excuse me / excusez-moi / eks-koo-zay mwa	
I'm very sorry / je suis désolé(e) / zhuh swee day-zo-lay	

— *extra vocabulary*

— *practice track number*

Office du Tourisme — Office de Tourisme

now practise   (3)
> le, la, les, un, une, des

blue CD2 track number

extra tip

examples in use

(6) Days of the week

Days of the week are masculine and are not written with a capital letter in French. The French for 'day' is le jour.

Monday	lundi / luñ-dee	Friday	vendredi / voñ-druh-dee
Tuesday	mardi / mar-dee	Saturday	samedi / sam-dee
Wednesday	mercredi / mehr-kruh-dee	Sunday	dimanche / dee-moñsh
Thursday	jeudi / zhuh-dee		

need to know
Le weekend **is one of the most established borrowings in French, as in** bon weekend!

To say that something happens on Monday, you just use the name of the day on its own:
je l'ai vu lundi I saw him on Monday
mercredi je vais à Paris on Wednesday I'm going to Paris
If you add the definite article le lundi you mean every Monday, on Mondays:
je la vois le lundi I see her on Mondays
The article is also used when giving a range of days:
du lundi 17 au vendredi 28 janvier from Monday 17 to Friday 28 January

every Monday	tous les lundis / too lay luñ-dee
last Tuesday	mardi dernier / mar-dee dehrn-yay
next Friday	vendredi prochain / voñ-druh-dee pro-shañ
a week on Saturday	samedi en huit / sam-dee oñ weet
today/tomorrow/yesterday	aujourd'hui/demain/hier / oh-zhoor-dwee/duh-mañ/yehr

112 | Speak French

Reference Zone

There are 33 tracks. You could think of it as a databank containing grammar, verb tables, numbers, days, months, times and so on. Each topic has a separate track. CD2 is useful for revision: it allows you to go back and choose what to practise, and it can also be used without referring to the book.

On the CD you hear a selection of the words and phrases shown in the book, as well as the most important tenses from the verb tables.

At the tourist office

get to know ...

> plurals
> masculine and feminine
> negatives
> accents

Caroline **Bonjour monsieur, je voudrais visiter le château demain et j'ai besoin d'un hôtel pour cette nuit. Il y a un hôtel ici?**
boñ-zhoor muhss-yuh, zhuh voo-dray vee-zee-tay luh sha-toh duh-mañ ay zhay buhz-wañ duñn o-tel poor set nwee. eel ee a uñn o-tel ee-see?
Hello, I'd like to visit the château tomorrow and I need a hotel for tonight. Is there a hotel here?

Employé **Oui madame, l'Hôtel de la Gare est à cinq minutes d'ici. Il faut aller au centre-ville**
wee ma-dam, loh-tel duh la gar ayt a sañ mee-noot dee-see. eel foh a-lay oh soñ-truh-veel
Yes, the Hôtel de la Gare (Station Hotel) is five minutes from here. You have to go to the centre of town

Caroline **Est-ce qu'on peut y aller à pied? Vous avez un plan de la ville?**
ess koñ puh ee a-lay a pyay? vooz a-vay uñ ploñ duh la veel?
Can you get there on foot? Have you got a streetmap?

Employé **Ce n'est pas loin. Voilà le plan**
suh nay pa lwañ. vwa-la luh ploñ
It's not far. Here's the map

Caroline **C'est combien?**
say koñb-yañ?
How much is it?

Employé **Rien, c'est gratuit**
ryañ, say gra-twee
Nothing, it's free

Caroline **Ah, merci beaucoup. Au revoir**
a, mehr-see boh-koo. oh ruh-vwar
Oh, thanks very much. Goodbye

More than one

Adding an -s is the standard way to make a plural in French: une minute, deux minutes. Adding the 's' doesn't affect how the word is pronounced. However, you have to remember to make the le and la plural. They both become les (*lay*) which no longer gives any clue to the gender. As in all things, there are exceptions: see the following noun endings -eau, -eu or -al (le bateau-les bateaux, le neveu-les neveux, le cheval-les chevaux). And nouns ending in -s, -x, or -z don't change in the plural. > NOUNS REFZONE 9.

It's a girl!

You'll probably be familiar with the concept of words being masculine (le plan) or feminine (la ville). This is known as 'gender', but it shouldn't be confused with the sex of humans or animals. Although words for things that are male or female in real life usually have the corresponding gender, you can't rely on it. To find out the gender of a word you will need to look it up in a dictionary, though sometimes you can make an educated guess from the ending. > NOUNS REFZONE 9.

What's in the article?

Le, la and les (meaning 'the') are known as definite articles. The indefinite ones meaning 'a' or 'an' or 'some' are un (for masculine nouns), une (for feminine nouns) and des (for both masculine and feminine). The important thing to remember is that des can never be missed out in French, even if there is no corresponding word in English. 'I bought apples and oranges' is much the same as 'I bought some apples and oranges', but in French you have to say j'ai acheté des pommes et des oranges.

from the dialogue

je voudrais ...
zhuh voo-dray ...
I'd like ...

demain
duh-mañ
tomorrow

j'ai besoin de ...
zhay buhz-wañ duh ...
I need ...

cette nuit
set nwee
tonight

il y a ...
eel ee a ...
there is/are ...

ici
ee-see
here

il faut ...
eel foh ...
you have to ...

vous avez ... ?
vooz a-vay ... ?
have you got ... ?

voilà
vwa-la
here you are

c'est combien?
say koñb-yañ?
how much is it?

rien
ryañ
nothing

c'est gratuit
say gra-twee
it's free

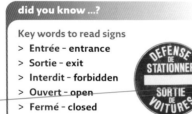

Greeting the day

The word bonjour literally means 'good day', but is equivalent to 'good morning' or 'good afternoon'. It's used until about 5pm, after which you can switch to bonsoir. Note that you can't say bon après-midi to mean 'good afternoon', since that would not be a greeting so much as an instruction to 'have a good afternoon'. And while in English 'goodnight' can be said as a night-time farewell, bonne nuit is for when someone is actually going to bed 'night-night!' To say goodbye at night, use bonsoir 'good evening'.

Not so

You probably know how to construct a negative in French: the verb must be enclosed between the two magic words ne and pas, for example je ne parle pas anglais 'I don't speak English'. In this dialogue we see how the ne abbreviates to n' before a vowel: c'est loin? 'is it far?' Non, ce n'est pas loin. 'No, it's not far'.

Little old I

In French capital letters aren't used as much as in English. 'I am' in English is always written with a capital I, but je suis in French is always with a lower-case j.

Vanishing vowels

Note that je becomes j' before a word starting with a vowel or, in most cases, h: j'ai 'I have'. It's the same with le and la, which both get reduced to l' in front of French words beginning with a vowel or, in most cases, the letter h: l'animal 'the animal', l'hôtel 'the hotel'. This is known as elision.

Yes, yes, yes

When someone offers you something, simply replying merci can be misleading. Depending on the tone of your voice, it can mean 'yes please' or 'no thank you'. Make sure you stress – oui, merci or non, merci. Otherwise you might not get that second helping you were offered! Or use the phrase merci, je veux bien (*mehr-see, zhuh vuh byañ*) – something like 'yes please I'd like that'.

Accentuate the difference

Here are the accents you will find in French: é (acute), è (grave), ê (circumflex), ë (diaresis) and ç (cedilla, only found with the letter c). Usually accents affect the pronunciation of a word, but not always. Some are there to distinguish two common words that would otherwise be identical in writing as well as pronunciation. Examples include ou 'or' and où 'where'; la 'the' (feminine definite article) and là 'there'; and sur 'on, on top of' and sûr 'sure'.

à la cafétéria

Spécial enfants

menu

Boîtakado

1 steak haché ou
3 bâtonnets de colin pané,
des frites, 1 dessert,
1 boisson,
1 gadget,
1 surprise !

3€ 80

GRATUIT LE MARDI SOIR *

Yes siree!

Remember to use those words monsieur and madame, that don't really have equivalents in British English. They're ideal when you don't know someone's name, whether it be someone you're introduced to, or just a stranger behind a desk at the tourist office. It doesn't sound excessively formal, as it might in English to use 'sir' or 'madam', all the time, and they can make your French sound more authentic.

now practise

3

> le, la, les, un, une, des

extra vocabulary

yes	**no**
oui	**non**
wee	*noñ*
ok!	**perhaps**
d'accord!	**peut-être**
da-kor!	*puht-etr*
please	
s'il vous plaît	
seel voo play	
thanks very much	
merci beaucoup	
mehr-see boh-koo	
hello (*day*)	**hello** (*evening*)
bonjour	**bonsoir**
boñ-zhoor	*boñ-swar*
goodbye	
au revoir	
oh ruh-vwar	
hi/bye	
salut	
sa-loo	
sorry/excuse me	
pardon	
par-doñ	
excuse me	
excusez-moi	
eks-koo-zay mwa	
I'm very sorry	
je suis désolé(e)	
zhuh swee day-zo-lay	

A chance encounter

get to know ...

> formal **vous**
> adjectives
> questions
> verbs

Mme Brun **Bonjour Madame Seguin. Comment allez-vous?**
boñ-zhoor ma-dam suh-gañ. ko-moñt alay voo?
Hello Mrs Seguin. How are you?

Mme Seguin **Bien merci. Et vous?**
byañ mehr-see. ay voo?
Fine thanks. And you?

Mme Brun **Très bien, je vous remercie. Et votre mari, comment va-t-il?**
tray byañ, zhuh voo ruh-mehr-see. ay vot-ruh ma-ree, ko-moñ va-teel?
Very well, thank you (I thank you). And your husband, how's he?

Mme Seguin **Il va bien, merci. Il repeint la cuisine ce week-end. Et vos enfants, ils vont bien?**
eel va byañ, mehr-see. eel ruh-pañ la kwee-zeen suh wee-kend. ay vohz oñ-foñ, eel voñ byañ?
He's fine, thanks. He's painting the kitchen this weekend. And your children, are they well?

Mme Brun **Oh, oui, ils vont très bien. Ils sont en vacances en ce moment**
oh wee, eel voñ tray byañ. eel soñt oñ va-koñss oñ suh mo-moñ
Oh yes, they're very well. They're on holiday at the moment

Mme Seguin **Bon, je dois filer. Bonne journée!**
boñ, zhuh dwa fee-lay. bon zhoor-nay!
Well, I must be going. Have a nice day!

Mme Brun **Merci, et vous de même. Au revoir, Madame Seguin!**
mehr-see, ay voo duh mem. oh ruh-vwar, ma-dam suh-gañ!
Thanks, and you too. Goodbye Mrs Seguin!

Mme Seguin **Au revoir!**
oh-ruh-vwar!
Goodbye!

Call me madame

We've already pointed out that the French use madame and monsieur much more than we do 'sir' and 'madam' in English, especially British English. When they are used with someone's surname, like 'Mr' and 'Mrs' in English, they are usually abbreviated when writing names to M and Mme. There is also mademoiselle for unmarried women, abbreviated to Mlle in names, though this is used less than it once was. If in doubt about someone's marital status, or to show respect to an older woman even if she is unmarried, the tendency is to address her as madame rather than mademoiselle.

Why so formal?

The two ladies use the formal word vous to each other. This is the polite form which you use with older people, or people you don't know very well, such as people working in shops. With your friends and family, as well as children, you use the less formal tu (see the next dialogue for the use of tu). But in the plural there's no choice, it's vous for everyone.

from the dialogue

comment allez-vous?
ko-moñt a-lay voo?
how are you?

bien merci
byañ mehr-see
fine thanks

je vous remercie
zhuh voo ru-mehr-see
thank you

comment va-t-il?
ko-moñ va-teel?
how is he?

il va bien
eel va byañ
he's ok

ce week-end
suh wee-kend
this weekend

en ce moment
oñ suh mo-moñ
at the moment

ils vont très bien
eel voñ tray byañ
they're very well

en vacances
oñ va-koñss
on holiday

je dois filer
zhuh dwa fee-lay
I must be going

bonne journée!
bon zhoor-nay!
have a nice day!

vous de même!
voo duh mem!
the same to you!

Begging the question

When someone asks you a question and you want to ask them the same thing back, it's easy. You just say et vous? literally, 'and you?' – or et toi? if it's someone you'd use tu with. This also works where you make a statement about yourself and want to ask the same of them: j'aime le football, et toi? 'I like football, do you?'

4

Coming to an agreement

Adjectives 'agree' by reflecting the noun they describe. For example, to make vert 'green' feminine, you add -e. To make vert plural, you add either -s (for masculine plural) or -es (for feminine plural). Where the adjective ends in -e already, it stays the same for both masculine and feminine eg pauvre, 'poor'. So bon 'good' becomes bonne when it goes with the feminine noun journée. We'll see plenty more of this later on. > ADJECTIVES REFZONE 10.

Goodwill gestures

To reply to some expression of goodwill such as the very common bonne journée 'have a nice day' you can use the phrase vous aussi or vous de même 'you too'. You can also use it as a reply to bon appétit 'enjoy your meal!', provided that the person who wishes it is also eating.

Meilleurs Vœux

Que cette nouvelle année
soit messagère de joie
de bonheur et de Paix

The longest day

Notice the two different words for 'day' – jour (as in bonjour) and journée (as in bonne journée)? There are other words where that added -ée can crop up, for example an/année 'year' and soir/soirée 'evening'. The effect is to emphasize the actual duration of a span of time, and it's often used in set expressions to wish someone a good something: bonne soirée! 'have a nice evening!', bonne année! 'happy new year!', etc. Notice that the form with -ée is feminine (le jour/la journée).

He sells, she sells

Notice how the French verb changes according to who is doing the action: je vais, il va, ils vont. This happens less in English, where we have only two forms for most verbs, eg 'I/you/we/they go', but 'he/she/it goes'. > ALLER (to go) REFZONE 25.

Er, well, anyway, y'know …

Every language has conversational 'fillers', little words or expression that are used not so much for their literal meaning as to fill a gap or move the conversation in a certain direction. Bon! says Mme Seguin, as she prepares to take her leave; 'right then!' we might say in English, or 'anyway …'.

Questions, questions, questions

There are a number of different ways of asking questions in French.

1 You can use the 'interrogative' (question) phrase est-ce que, for example est-ce que vous avez … ? 'do you have …?' This is probably the one you remember from school days.
2 You can turn verb and subject around (inversion), avez-vous … ? Notice that you add a hyphen between verb and subject.
3 Finally, you can just use the pitch of your voice (intonation) by rising at the end of the phrase: vous avez … ? 'do you have … ?'
> QUESTIONS REFZONE 15.

The imposters

Although the French authorities try to keep English out, there are some words that just refuse to stay away. These include: le jean, le hamburger, le whisky and le week-end. Some words are a combination of American or abbreviations of the original word: les baskets 'trainers', le slip 'underpants', le stop 'hitch-hiking', le pull 'pullover' and le foot 'football' as well as le footing 'jogging'.

Meeting an old friend

get to know ...

> informal **tu**
> negatives without **ne**
> telling the time
> possessives

Alain **Tiens, salut Bruno! Comment vas-tu?**
tyañ, sa-loo broo-noh! ko-moñ va too?
Hey, hi Bruno! How are you?

(they shake hands)

Bruno **Salut Alain. Bien, merci. Et toi?**
sa-loo a-lañ! byañ mehr-see. ay twa?
Hi Alain. Fine, thanks. What about you?

Alain **Ouais, pas mal, merci. Je suis en congés en ce moment**
way, pa mal mehr-see. zhuh swee oñ koñ-zhay oñ suh mo-moñ
Yeah, not bad, thanks. I'm off work at the moment

Bruno **Tu veux aller prendre un verre? Je retourne au boulot dans une heure**
too vuh a-lay proñ-druh uñ vehr? zhuh ruh-toorn oh boo-loh doñz oon uhr
Would you like to go and have a drink? I'm going back to work in an hour

Alain **Oui, pourquoi pas? C'est pas mal comme idée. J'ai rendez-vous avec ma mère à six heures, alors j'ai le temps**
wee, poor-kwa pa? say pa mal kom ee-day. zhay roñ-day-voo a-vek ma mehr a seez uhr, a-lor zhay luh toñ
Yes, why not? That's not a bad idea. I am meeting my mum at six, so I've got time

Bruno **On va au café sur la place? Allez, je t'invite!**
oñ va oh ka-fay soor la plass? a-lay, zhuh tañ-veet!
Shall we go to the cafe in the square? Go on, I'm paying!

(a little later)

Alain **Merci pour la bière. À bientôt!**
mehr-see poor la byehr. a byañ-toh!
Thanks for the beer. See you soon!

Bruno **Je t'en prie. Allez, bonne soirée!**
zhuh toñ pree. a-lay, bon swa-ray!
You're welcome. Well, have a good evening!

Among friends

You'll notice that Bruno and Alain don't use the vous form with each other as the two ladies in the previous dialogue did. They use the informal tu, partly because they are good friends and also because they are younger and less formal than Mme Seguin and Mme Brun. You can see this informality throughout the conversation in their choice of expressions like salut 'hi' instead of bonjour. However, they would use vous with the waiter.

Mwah mwah

The boys shake hands when they meet. This is a routine greeting for French people and not just a thing you do when meeting someone for the first time. If it were two female friends, or one of each sex, they would kiss each other on the cheek, anywhere between two and four times, according to the tradition of the area – both on meeting and departing! – although they would still shake hands when first introduced.

from the dialogue

tiens!
tyañ!
hey!

comment vas-tu?
ko-moñ va too?
how are you?

pas mal
pa mal
not bad

je suis en congés
zhuh swee oñ koñ-zhay
I'm off work

prendre un verre
proñ-druh uñ vehr
to have a drink

au boulot
oh boo-loh
at work

dans une heure
doñz oon uhr
in an hour

pourquoi pas?
poor-kwa pa?
why not?

j'ai le temps
zhay luh toñ
I have time

je t'en prie
zhuh toñ pree
don't mention it

allez!
a-lay
go on!

bonne soirée!
bon swa-ray!
have a good evening!

Eliminate the negative

As we've seen, this is an informal dialogue. They use words like ouais (an informal pronunciation of oui, equivalent to our 'yeah' for 'yes') and boulot for 'work' or 'job'. One major characteristic of informal everyday speech that you will soon start to notice is the way people simplify the negative construction by dropping the ne part, eg je (ne) suis pas d'ici 'I'm not from here'. So instead of ce n'est pas mal 'it's not bad' we just have c'est pas mal.

My word

You might not think it, but 'your', 'my', 'his' are also adjectives, known in the grammatical world as possessive adjectives, because they show who possesses the noun. So 'my mum' is ma mère. The tricky bit in French is that 'my', 'your', 'his', etc, have to agree with what they're describing, not with the owner of the thing as they do in English. It might be 'his car', but as car is feminine in French, the adjective has to show its feminine side, so it's sa voiture not son voiture. > Possessives RefZone 11.

What hour is it?

In telling the time, the English expression 'o'clock' is rendered using the word heure 'hour'. Quelle heure est-il? 'what time is it?' il est six heures 'it's six o'clock'. Note that heure is feminine, so when it comes to half past the hour, you will need to add an -e to the demi: une heure et demie 'half past one'. But a half-hour period, 'half an hour', is a set phrase without the -e: une demi-heure.
> Time RefZone 4.

Taking the waters

When choosing food and drink, or purchases in a shop, remember to use the verb prendre. In English – modern English at least – we say 'to have a drink' or 'I'll have the lasagne' but in French you 'take' the thing specified: tu veux prendre un verre? 'would you like to have a drink?'; je prends une bière 'I'll have a beer'.

In the street, but on the square

Another case where French usage differs slightly is in the choice of preposition – the little words that introduce a noun. For example, 'in the street' or 'on the street' – either is possible in English nowadays. But you would say 'in the square', rather than 'on the square', which is what French says: le café sur la place. Other examples are sur le marché 'at (on) the market'and sur le parking 'in the car park'. > PREPOSITIONS REFZONE 14.

Go do it! Come and get it!

In English we often use 'and' with the verbs 'come' and 'go', in such phrases as 'I'll go and see if he's ready', 'come and have a drink'. In some cases 'to' is also possible. But in French no extra word is needed, just the infinitive (the part of the verb that doesn't specify who's doing the action). Tu viens prendre un verre? 'are you coming for (to take) a drink?' Notice that you can also put two infinitives together, as we see here: tu veux aller prendre un verre? 'do you want to go (and) have a drink?'

Till soon!

When in English we would say 'see you ... ' (soon, next week, on Monday, etc) in French you just use the word à, here meaning something like 'until'. Two common examples are à bientôt! 'see you soon!' and au revoir 'goodbye!', more literally 'till we see each other again' – here the à has combined with le (le revoir 'the seeing again') to give au. You can put just about anything into this structure: à la semaine prochaine, à lundi, au mois prochain! 'see you next week/on Monday/next month'.

now practise

7

> negatives

---

extra vocabulary

one	eleven
un(e)	onze
uñ(oon)	*oñz*
two	twelve
deux	douze
duh	*dooz*
three	thirteen
trois	treize
trwa	*trez*
four	fourteen
quatre	quatorze
kat-ruh	*ka-torz*
five	fifteen
cinq	quinze
sañk	*kañz*
six	sixteen
six	seize
seess	*sez*
seven	seventeen
sept	dix-sept
set	*dee-set*
eight	eighteen
huit	dix-huit
weet	*dee-weet*
nine	nineteen
neuf	dix-neuf
nuhf	*deez-nuhf*
ten	twenty
dix	vingt
deess	*vañ*

Asking the way

get to know ...

> directions
> numbers
> il faut
> devoir

Caroline **Excusez-moi madame. Je cherche le musée des Beaux-Arts, mais je suis un peu perdue**
eks-koo-zay-mwa ma-dam. zhuh shehrsh luh moo-zay day boh-zar, may zhuh swee uñ puh pehr-doo
Excuse me. I'm looking for the Museum of Fine Art, but I'm a bit lost

Mme Seguin **Ah, le musée des Beaux-Arts? C'est facile! Prenez la première rue à gauche, continuez tout droit jusqu'aux feux, puis tournez à droite dans la rue Carnot, et le musée est juste en face**
ah, luh moo-zay day boh-zar? say fa-seel! pruh-nay la pruhm-yehr roo a gohsh, koñ-tee-noo-ay too drwa joosk-oh fuh, pwee toor-nay a drwat doñ la roo kar-noh, ay luh moo-zay ay joost oñ fass
Ah, the Museum of Fine Art? It's easy! Take the first road on the left, then keep going straight on until the traffic lights, then turn right into Carnot Street, and the museum is right opposite

Caroline **Ah, vous parlez trop vite pour moi! Vous pouvez répéter, s'il vous plaît?**
a, voo par-lay troh veet poor mwa! voo poo-vay ray-pay-tay, seel voo play?
Oh, you're speaking too fast for me! Can you repeat that please?

Mme Seguin **Donc, la première à gauche, tout droit puis à droite après les feux, et c'est en face**
doñk, la pruhm-yehr a gohsh, too drwa pwee a drawt a-pray lay fuh, ay sayt oñ fass
So, it's the first on the left, straight on then right after the lights, and it's opposite

Caroline **Merci. C'est loin?**
mehr-see. say lwañ?
Thanks. Is it far?

Mme Seguin **Non, c'est à cinq minutes d'ici à pied**
noñ, sayt a sañ mee-noot dee-see a pyay
No, it's five minutes from here on foot

Caroline Très bien, merci. Et j'ai aussi entendu parler du musée de la science. Il est où? Est-ce qu'il est dans le même quartier?

tray byañ, mehr-see. ay zhay oh-see oñ-toñ-doo par-lay doo moo-zay duh la see-oñss. eel ay oo? ess keel ay doñ luh mem kart-yay?

Great, thanks. And I've also heard about the science museum. Where is it? Is it in the same area?

Mme Seguin Ah non, il est de l'autre côté de la ville. Il faut y aller en bus ou en voiture

a noñ, eel ay duh loh-truh ko-tay duh la veel. eel foh ee a-lay oñ boos oo oñ vwa-toor

Ah no, it is on the other side of town. You have to get there by bus or by car

Caroline Bon, je le visiterai peut-être demain

boñ, zhuh luh vee-zee-tray puh-tetr duh-mañ

Well, perhaps I'll visit it tomorrow

Pardon my French!

The phrase excusez-moi! is one way of getting someone's attention, just like the English 'excuse me!' You can also say pardon!, or just use monsieur! or madame! as appropriate. Pardon? can also be used to ask someone to repeat something.

Where is ... ?

Asking for directions is one of the most important things you need to do when abroad. As well as the straightforward où est ... you can just name the place you want and add ... c'est où? 'where is it?' Or, as here, you can say that you're 'looking for' the place in question: je cherche ... .

This and that

The word for both 'this' and 'that' is ce (cette for feminine singular, cet for masculine nouns beginning with a vowel or, in most cases, the letter h, ces for masculine or feminine plural). In fact ce often means something nearer to 'the' than 'this'. To make things clearer you can add either -ci 'this' or -là 'that' to the end of the noun: ce modèle-ci 'this model, not that one', cette carte-ci 'this card here'.
> Demonstratives RefZone 12.

Planes, trains and automobiles

Here are some different ways of getting around. While we say 'by … ' in English, French mostly uses 'en … ': en avion 'by plane', en bateau 'by boat', en voiture 'by car', en train 'by train', en autobus 'by bus' – but à pied 'on foot' and à vélo 'by bike'.

Should, ought to

Remember that verb devoir 'must, have to'? Here we find it in the conditional tense, vous devriez – literally 'you would have to' – which means 'you ought to, you should'.
> Devoir (to have to) RefZone 26.

Il faut …

This is often translated as 'it is necessary to … ', although in English we might more naturally phrase it with 'have to' or 'need to'. Here we have il faut y aller en bus 'you have to get there by bus'. More on this useful construction at Dialogue 26.

The numbers game

Numbers come in two sorts. There are the ones you use for saying how many of something there is, eg cinq minutes 'five minutes', and the ones that help you put things in order: la première/deuxième/ troisième rue à gauche, 'the first/second/ third street on the left'. In English it goes one–first, two–second, three–third, four–fourth and so on. In French it's slightly simpler. You make the second kind out of the first by adding -ième, except for 'first' which is premier (première in the feminine).
> Numbers RefZone 3.

The bright lights

The word for 'traffic light' is the same as for 'fire': le feu.
The usual way of making a plural (to refer to more than one of
something) is to add an –s. But there are irregular plurals, and
sometimes the plural is invariable, in other words the plural is the
same as the singular and nothing is added (le bus, les bus, le prix,
les prix). Feu takes –x, quite a common irregular plural ending:
jusqu'aux feux 'as far as the lights'. > NOUNS REFZONE 9.

extra vocabulary

in the square
sur la place
soor la plass

in the street
dans la rue
doñ la roo

at the market
sur le marché
soor luh mar-shay

in front of the station
devant la gare
duh-voñ la gar

behind the garage
derrière le garage
dehr-yehr luh ga-razh

at the cash desk
à la caisse
a la kess

at the counter
au guichet
oh gee-shay

near the beach
près de la plage
pray duh la plazh

in the village
dans le village
doñ luh vee-lazh

after the traffic lights
après les feux
a-pray lay fuh

in the car park
sur le parking
soor luh par-keeng

now practise

9

> **understanding directions**

At a café

Serveuse **Qu'est-ce que je vous sers?**
kess-kuh zhuh voo sehr?
What can I get you?

Alain **Un crème, s'il vous plaît. Pierre, qu'est-ce que tu prends?**
uñ krem, seel voo play. pyehr, kess kuh too proñ?
A white coffee, please. Pierre, what are you having?

Pierre **Une bouteille d'eau minérale**
oon boo-tay doh mee-nay-ral
A bottle of mineral water

Serveuse **Plate ou gazeuse?**
plat oo ga-zuhz?
Still or sparkling?

Pierre **Gazeuse, s'il vous plaît. Et avec des glaçons**
ga-zuhz, seel voo play. ay a-vek day gla-soñ
Sparkling, please. And with ice

Serveuse **Alors ... voilà un crème et une eau gazeuse**
a-lor ... vwa-la uñ krem ay oon oh ga-zuhz
So ... here you are, a white coffee and a sparkling water

Alain **Vous avez des sucrettes?**
vooz a-vay day soo-kret?
Do you have any sweeteners?

Serveuse **Je vais en chercher. Ce sera tout?**
zhuh vay oñ shehr-shay. suh suh-ra too?
I'll go and get some. Is that everything?

Alain **Et un autre crème, s'il vous plaît. Ça fait combien en tout?**
ay uñn oh-truh krem, seel voo play. sa fay koñ-byañ oñ too?
And another white coffee, please. How much is that altogether?

Serveuse **Cinq euros cinquante**
sañk uh-roh sañ-koñt
five euros fifty

BRASSERIE LE FRANÇAIS

from the dialogue

qu'est-ce que tu prends?
kess kuh too proñ?
what are you having?

une bouteille d'eau minérale
oon boo-tay doh mee-nay-ral
a bottle of mineral water

plate
plat
still

gazeuse
ga-zuhz
sparkling

des glaçons
day gla-soñ
some ice

des sucrettes
day soo-kret
some sweeteners

je vais en chercher
zhuh vay oñ shehr-shay
I'll go and get some

un autre crème
un oh-truh krem
another white coffee

ça fait combien en tout?
sa fay koñ-byañ oñ too?
how much is that altogether?

All about en

The word en is everywhere – it has so many meanings! We've already seen how to use it to refer to location (en France 'in or to France'), means of transport (en voiture 'by car') materials (en verre 'made of glass'), activity or state (en vacances 'on holiday', en congés 'off work', en retard 'late') and various other expressions such as en plus 'as well' and en tout 'in total'. But en has another major function: taking the place of an expression involving de, to avoid repeating the same word. In exchanges like vous avez des sucrettes? – je vais en chercher 'do you have any sweeteners? – I'll go and get some', en replaces des sucrettes (in je vais chercher des sucrettes); in je voudrais des pommes – vous en voulez combien? 'I'd like some apples – how many do you want?', en replaces des pommes (in vous voulez combien de pommes?). So you can think of the en as representing 'of it, of them'.

Sounding off

Note that with many adjectives, there is a change not just in the spelling but in the pronunciation; the added -e causes a consonant to be pronounced that was silent in the masculine form – in eau plate 'still water' the t is pronounced (*oh plat*), though it's silent in the masculine form plat (*pla*); and eau gazeuse 'sparkling water' takes on a final z sound (*oh ga-zuhz*) that is not heard in the masculine gazeux (*ga-zuh*).

Getting your words in order

You'll have noticed by now, if you didn't know already, that there is also a difference from English in the word order. Generally speaking, adjectives (gazeux, 'sparkling') come after the noun (eau, 'water') in French. But there are some very common adjectives that break this rule, and usually come before the noun they refer to.

Here are some of that select group of adjectives that normally come before rather than after the noun: beau 'beautiful', bon 'good', mauvais 'bad', gentil 'nice', grand 'large', gros 'big', petit 'small', long 'long', jeune 'young', vieux 'old', meilleur 'better, best', pire 'worse, worst'.

Sometimes the word order even makes a difference to the meaning. For example, ancien means 'old' in the sense of 'ancient' when it comes after the noun (une ville ancienne 'an old town'), but old in the sense of 'former' when it comes before (mon ancien professeur 'my old teacher'). > ADJECTIVES REFZONE 10.

With or without

Note that there are cases where an article is optional in English, but essential in French: 'with ice' is much the same as 'with some ice', but in French you have to say avec des glaçons. When you are referring to all examples of a thing, seen collectively as a category, English uses the word on its own 'I like oranges/football' but in French you need the definite article: j'aime les oranges/ le football.

Farewell franc!

France is in the eurozone. The word euro is masculine. The subdivisions, called cents in English, are known as centimes in France, but just as with pounds and pence, you often don't need to use the word: €1.50 is un euro cinquante, etc.

How to order and pay in a café
In a traditional café it's common to run a tab and pay when you are about to leave, as you would for a meal. However at busy places or times they may ask you to pay straight away. A useful phrase for asking 'how much is that?' is ça fait combien? – literally 'how much does that make?'

Coffee

The standard type of coffee in France (un café) is an espresso: small, strong and black. If you prefer to have more coffee, but less strong, ask for un café rallongé. If you want a white coffee you should ask for un café crème (or just un crème for short). This is the French equivalent to a cappuccino but it can still be quite small so you might like to ask for un grand crème. A café au lait is a strong black coffee served with milk (usually warm), separately. If you ask for a cappuccino you find that it usually comes with a dollop of whipped cream on top.

What's ça?

You may not be familiar with the little accent looking like a number 5 stuck to the bottom of the letter c. It's called a cedilla, and it marks a case when the c is pronounced 'soft' like an s rather than 'hard' like a k. This is necessary because by default the letter c is 'hard' before the vowels a, o and u, and 'soft' only when followed by e, i or y. Thus, it's ici 'here' but ça 'that'; ancien 'old, former' but français 'French'. A cedilla also came with the ice (avec des glaçons).

extra vocabulary

a glass of red wine
un verre de vin rouge
uñ vehr duh vañ roozh

a cup of tea
une tasse de thé
oon tass duh tay

some red wine
du vin rouge
doo vañ roozh

some white wine
du vin blanc
doo vañ bloñ

the house wine
la cuvée du patron
la koo-vay doo pa-troñ

a carafe of red wine
un pichet de vin rouge
uñ pee-shay duh vañ roozh

a half of lager
un demi
uñ duh-mee

draught lager
une (bière) pression
oon (byehr) press-yoñ

a jug of water
une carafe d'eau
oon ka-raff doh

still water
de l'eau plate
duh loh plat

sparkling water
de l'eau gazeuse
duh loh gah-zuhz

Making friends

get to know ...

> giving your name and age
> reflexive verbs
> languages and nationalities
> prepositions

Amandine **Bonjour! Je m'appelle Amandine. Et toi, comment tu t'appelles?**
boñ-zhoor! zhuh ma-pel a-moñ-deen. ay twa, ko-moñ <u>too</u> ta-pel?
Hello! My name's Amandine. And you, what's your name?

Katy **Je m'appelle Katy. J'ai treize ans. Et toi, tu as quel âge?**
zhuh ma-pel Katy. zhay trez oñ. ay twa, <u>too</u> a kel azh?
My name is Katy. I'm 13 years old. How old are you?

Amandine **J'ai quatorze ans. Mon nom de famille, c'est Meunier. Tu habites ici?**
zhay kat-orz oñ. moñ noñ duh fa-mee say muhn-yay. <u>too</u> a-beet ee-see?
I'm 14. My surname is Meunier. Do you live here?

Katy **Non, je suis en vacances avec ma famille. On loue un appartement près de la plage**
noñ, zhuh sweez oñ va-koñss a-vek ma fa-mee. oñ loo uññ a-par-tuh-moñ pray duh la plazh
No, I'm on holiday with my family. We're renting a flat near the beach

Amandine **Tu es d'où?**
<u>too</u> ay doo?
Where are you from?

Katy **Je suis de Londres. Je suis anglaise. Et toi, tu habites ici?**
zhuh swee duh loñ-druh. zhuh swee oñ-glehz. ay twa, <u>too</u> a-beet ee-see?
I'm from London. I'm English. What about you, do you live here?

Amandine **Oui, j'habite à Calais, près du centre-ville. Et je suis française. J'apprends l'anglais à l'école mais je ne suis pas très bonne**
wee, zha-beet a ka-lay, pray doo soñtr-veel. ay zhuh swee froñ-sehz. zha-proñ loñ-glay a lay-kol may zhuh nuh swee pa tray bon
Yes, I live in Calais, near the centre of town. And I'm French. I am learning English at school but I'm not very good

Katy **Je ne parle pas très bien français non plus!**
zhuh nuh parl pa tray byañ froñ-say noñ <u>ploo</u>!
I don't speak French very well either!

Name-dropping

By default, nom 'name' tends to refer to a person's surname in French, otherwise known as nom de famille 'family name'. For first name you will see the word prénom. Look out for this on official forms. Giving your name is a good example of how word-for-word translations can lead you astray. Mon nom est ... might literally translate 'my name is ... ', but it's not what people usually say. To state your name you need to use the verb appeler 'to call' and a 'reflexive' construction where the action of the verb is done to oneself: je m'appelle Katy – literally, 'I call myself Katy'.

Lightning reflexes

Reflexive verbs are more common in French than in English. For example, you can say in English 'I washed myself'. But it sounds much more natural not to state who the washing happens to, and just say 'I washed', 'I shaved', etc. In French you have to remember to add the bit that refers to who is receiving the action, even when there doesn't seem to be any action performed on oneself. 'I'm interested in cars' is je m'intéresse aux voitures, literally 'I interest myself in cars'. Highly illogical, you may be thinking. But then, why should it be 'I enjoyed myself'? Sometimes you just have to answer 'because that's the way it is', and not worry about it too much. > Reflexive verbs RefZone 32.

Age concerns

In English we 'are' a certain age, in other words we use the verb 'to be' to give the age of a person or thing. In French people 'have' a certain age, using avoir 'to have': j'ai treize ans 'I'm thirteen (years old)' quel âge as-tu? 'how old are you?'. Note that the word for years (ans) is not optional as in English 'I'm 13', you must include it in French.

from the dialogue

je m'appelle ...
zhuh ma-pel ...
my name is ...

comment tu t'appelles?
ko-moñ too ta-pel?
what's your name?

j'ai treize ans
zhay trez oñ
I'm 13 years old

tu as quel âge?
too a kel azh?
how old are you?

mon nom de famille
moñ noñ duh fa-mee
my surname

tu habites ici?
too a-beet ee-see?
do you live here?

on loue un appartement
oñ loo uñn a-par-tuh-moñ
we're renting a flat

tu es d'où?
too ay doo?
where are you from?

je suis de Londres
zhuh swee duh loñ-druh
I'm from London

je suis anglaise
zhuh swee oñ-glez
I'm English

j'habite à Calais
zha-beet a ka-lay
I live in Calais

j'apprends l'anglais
zha-proñ loñ-glay
I'm learning English

The capital of France

In French as in English, countries have capital letters – la France. But the same is not true of languages – le français – or adjectives of nationality – français(e). Languages are masculine nouns, and look the same as the relevant adjective of nationality: il est français, il parle français; elle est anglaise, elle parle anglais etc. But the word for a French person *does* take a capital: un Français 'a Frenchman', une Anglaise 'an Englishwoman' etc. Contrast these sentences: il est français 'of French nationality' – c'est un Français 'a Frenchman'; le français est la langue française 'French (noun) is the French (adjective) language'. To put it another way, les Français sont français, ils parlent français 'the French (noun) are French (adjective), they speak French'. Not all nationalities end in -ais, however. Here are some different endings: américain 'American', canadien 'Canadian', gallois 'Welsh', belge 'Belgian', suisse 'Swiss', turc/turque 'Turkish', grec/grecque 'Greek'.

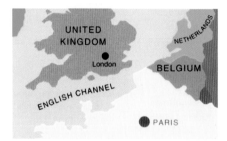

Be lucky

As we've seen, French sometimes uses a different verb to English, for example avoir 'to have' for people's ages, rather than être 'to be'. Same thing here: vous avez de la chance! 'you're in luck, you're lucky!' – literally, 'you have luck'. (Compare this with the use of faire in such expressions as vous faites quelle pointure? 'what size do you take?' and il fait chaud aujourd'hui 'it's hot today'.) As well as ages and luck, avoir is also used for being hungry and thirsty. In French you literally 'have' hunger (faim) or thirst (soif) – j'ai faim! Tu as soif? – and being right or wrong about something – tu as raison/tort.

Prepositions without tears

We've seen the phrase en vacances 'on holiday'. But how do you know it's going to be en rather than à or sur or anything else? The simple answer is, you probably don't. You could guess, but remember, not everything in language is logical or guessable! The best thing is just to learn which prepositions are right in which cases – which is why we give you phrases (en vacances) rather than expecting you to construct them from scratch.

> PREPOSITIONS REFZONE 14.

Getting contractions

When à is followed by le/les, the two combine to give au and aux respectively. À la stays as it is. The same kind of thing happens with de when it comes up against le and les: de+le=du, and de+les=des. However, when you're specifying an amount or containerful of something, for example une bouteille d'eau 'a bottle of water' or six tranches de jambon 'six slices of ham', you don't have the le/la/les part. So, not 'une bouteille de l'eau' here.

No place like home

It's essential to be able to say where you're from, where you're staying, where you're travelling to, and so on. You'll notice that in Calais is à Calais; we also have en Angleterre, en France and au Canada. In English you can say either 'at' or 'in' cities, though 'in' is more common today; French sticks to à for towns and cities and en for feminine countries (au for masculine), except in the few cases where the name of a city includes a definite article, as in le Havre 'the Havre' rather than just 'Havre', where 'at The Havre' is, logically enough, au Havre rather than à Havre. Where a place name is in the plural, for example in the case of island groups, we need aux (from à + le, see above), eg aux Îles Anglo-normandes 'in the Channel Islands'.

You say neither ...

We know about aussi 'as well, also'. The negative version of it, 'neither', is non plus: je ne parle pas très bien français non plus! I don't speak French very well either! Here are some more examples of aussi and non plus:

il parle français, et elle aussi
'he speaks French, and she does too'
je ne parle pas allemand – moi non plus! – elle non plus!
'I don't speak German – nor do I! – nor does she!'

now practise **13**

> asking questions

I'm Irish
je suis irlandais(e)
zhuh sweez eer-loñ-day(z)

we're Scottish
nous sommes écossais(es)
noo somz ay-ko-say(z)

she is English
elle est anglaise
el ayt oñ-glayz

he is Belgian
il est belge
eel ay belzh

are you Swiss?
êtes-vous suisse?
et-voo sweess

they are American
ils sont américains
eel soñt a-may-ree-kañ

she is American
elle est américaine
el ayt a-may-ree-ken

he is Canadian
il est canadien
eel ay ka-nad-yañ

she is Australian
elle est australienne
el ayt o-stral-yen

Meeting family

14

get to know ...

> diminutives
> impersonal on
> depuis
> weather

Amandine **Harry, je te présente ma grand-mère. Elle habite chez nous**
a-ree, zhuh tuh pray-zoñt ma groñ-mehr. el a-beet shay noo
Harry, let me introduce my grandmother (to you). She lives with us

Harry **Enchanté de faire votre connaissance, madame**
oñ-shoñ-tay duh fehr vo-truh ko-nay-soñss, ma-dam
Pleased to meet you

Mme Seguin **Alors, tu profites bien de tes vacances?**
a-lor, too pro-feet byañ duh tay va-koñss?
Well then, are you making the most of your holidays?

Harry **Oui, merci. Et comme il fait beau, je peux aller nager tous les jours**
wee, mehr-see. ay kom eel fay boh, zhuh puh a-lay na-zhay too lay zhoor
Yes, thanks. And as it's good weather, I can go swimming every day

Mme Seguin **Fais attention! Il fait très chaud en ce moment**
fay a-toñss-yoñ! eel fay tray shoh oñ suh mo-moñ
Be careful! It is very hot at the moment

Amandine **Mamie! On n'est plus des enfants!**
ma-mee! oñ nay ploo dayz oñ-foñ!
Granny! We're not children any more!

Harry **Oui, c'est vrai, il fait très chaud, mais je mets toujours de la crème solaire et je porte un chapeau**
wee, say vray, eel fay tray shoh, may zhuh may too-zhoor duh la krehm so-lehr ay zhuh port uñ sha-poh
Yes, it's true, it is very hot, but I always put suncream on and wear a hat

Mme Seguin **Tu parles bien français. Tu as appris à l'école?**
too parl byañ froñ-say. too a a-pree a lay-kol?
You speak French well. Did you learn at school?

Harry **Oui, j'apprends le français depuis trois ans**
wee, zha-proñ luh froñ-say duh-pwee trwaz oñ
Yes, I've been learning French for three years

Amandine **Bon eh bien, on va à la piscine maintenant.**
Au revoir, Mamie!
boñ ay byañ, oñ va a la pee-seen mañ-tuh-noñ.
oh ruh-vwar, ma-mee!
OK, well, we're off to the swimming-pool now.
Goodbye, granny!

Mme Seguin **Amusez-vous bien!**
a-moo-zay-voo byañ!
Have fun!

Harry **Au revoir, madame!**
oh ruh-vwar, ma-dam!
Goodbye!

from the dialogue

je te présente ...
zhuh tuh pray-zoñt ...
let me introduce ...

chez nous
shay noo
with us

enchanté de faire votre connaissance
oñ-shoñ-tay duh fehr vo-truh ko-nay-soñss
pleased to meet you

il fait beau
eel fay boh
it's good weather

tous les jours
too lay zhoor
every day

fais attention!
fay a-toñss-yoñ!
be careful!

il fait très chaud
eel fay tray shoh
it's very hot

depuis trois ans
duh-pwee trwaz oñ
for three years now

on va à la piscine
oñ va a la pee-seen
we're off to the pool

amusez-vous bien!
a-moo-zay-voo byañ!
have fun!

Little old lady

Granny, gran, grandma – every language has its 'diminutives', those little words that show affection or familiarity. As well as mamie 'grandma' you might come across maman 'mummy' and papa 'daddy'. An important difference with English is that these are only used (by adults at least) as a term of address, that is when speaking to the person concerned, not about them. In English you can refer to 'my dad', but mon papa in French would sound childish 'my daddy', and you should use mon père.

did you know ...?

Shoving it down their throats
When introducing people remember to use the verb présenter and not introduire, which means to introduce physically as in 'insert into' – you don't want to invoke any distressing mental images to your new friends!

Chez nous

You're probably already familiar with the the word chez which helps you state where someone lives or works or is based in whatever way. You just add the relevant person after the chez. Simple: chez nous 'at our house, where we live'; elle habite chez nous 'she lives with us'; chez Alain il y a une piscine 'there's a swimming-pool at Alain's place'; je vais chez le médecin 'I'm going to the doctor's'.

One does love swimming

You might see the pronoun on translated as 'one', but that's rather misleading as there are very important differences of tone and usage. The French use on (which doesn't sound in the least pompous, as 'one' can) in all sorts of situations when it's not necessary to specify exactly who does the action. It can mean people generally (en France on aime le vin rouge 'in France people – or 'we' or 'they' – like red wine'), but it's very often used, as here, to mean 'we'. On n'est plus des enfants! 'We're not children any more!' In the previous dialogue, Katy used the phrase on loue un appartement près de la plage, which really means no more than 'a flat near the beach is being rented', but in context clearly means 'we're renting a flat near the beach'. In this dialogue we have on va à la piscine 'we're going swimming' (literally 'going to the swimming-pool'). It's very useful for making suggestions, too. Just say the same sentence with a rising intonation – on va à la piscine? – and you have 'shall we go swimming'?

'For' and 'since'

In English you can say 'I've been learning French for three years', or 'I started learning French three years ago'. The first describes how long an action has been going on; the second says when the action started. In French the magic word covering 'for' and 'since' is depuis, and you use it with the present tense: j'apprends l'anglais depuis trois ans, literally 'I'm learning English since three years'. If that sounds like something a French speaker might say to you in their imperfect English, that's because they have trouble with this one too.

Fair weather

Whether it's good or bad, we all find ourselves talking about the weather. An important point to bear in mind is that while in English we say 'it is hot/cold/windy' etc, the French use the verb faire (usually translated as 'to do' or 'to make'): il fait chaud 'it's hot', il fait froid 'it's cold', il fait du vent 'it's windy'. If you want to intensify the temperature, as in this dialogue, you use très: il fait très chaud 'it's very hot'.

More on faire

As well as weather, faire is used in quite a few expressions where you might not expect it. In English we say to pay attention, but in French it's faire attention. To meet someone for the first time is to make their acquaintance: faire la connaissance de quelqu'un. Other examples include faire des achats 'to go shopping', faire une promenade 'to go for a walk', faire un voyage 'to go on a journey' and faire la queue 'to queue up'.

extra vocabulary

it's raining
il pleut
eel pluh

it's snowing
il neige
eel nezh

it's windy
il fait du vent
eel fay doo voñ

it's foggy
il fait du brouillard
eel fay doo broo-yar

it's hot
il fait chaud
eel fay shoh

it's cold
il fait froid
eel fay frwa

what a lovely day!
qu'est-ce qu'il fait beau!
kess keel fay boh!

the weather is awful
il fait un temps affreux
eel fayt uñ toñ a-fruh

storm
l'orage
lo-razh

snow
la neige
la nezh

hail
la grêle
la grel

now practise

> **understanding weather forecast**

At a restaurant

get to know ...

> quel
> commands
> comme
> bon and bien

Alain **Bonsoir. Une table pour deux personnes, s'il vous plaît**
boñ-swahr. <u>oo</u>n tabl poor duh per-son, seel voo play
Hello. A table for two, please

Serveur **Je vous mets près de la fenêtre. Installez-vous. Voilà la carte**
zhuh voo may pray duh la fuh-netr. añ-sta-lay voo. vwa-la la kart
I'll put you near the window. Please sit down. Here is the menu

(later)

Serveur **vous avez choisi?**
vooz a-vay shwa-zee?
Have you chosen?

Delphine **Non, pas encore. Je suis végétarienne; quels plats me conseillez-vous?**
noñ, pa oñ-kor. zhuh swee vay-zhay-tar-yen; kel pla muh koñ-say-ay-voo?
No, not yet. I'm a vegetarian – what dishes would you recommend to me?

Serveur **Alors, en entrée nous avons une terrine de légumes, et comme plat principal vous pouvez prendre la ratatouille**
a-lor, oñn oñ-tray nooz a-voñ <u>oo</u>n te-reen duh lay-g<u>oo</u>m, ay kom pla prañ-see-pal voo poo-vay proñ-druh la ra-ta-too-ee
Well, for a starter we have a vegetable pâté and for a main course you could have the ratatouille

Delphine **Oui, très bien, c'est ce que je vais prendre. Et toi chéri, qu'est-ce que tu prends?**
wee, tray byañ, say suh kuh zhuh vay proñdr. ay twa she-ree, kess kuh too proñ?
Yes, very good, that's what I'll have. And you, dear, what will you have?

Alain **Alors moi, je vais prendre le menu à douze euros. La soupe du jour, c'est quoi?**
a-lor mwa, zhuh vay proñdr luh muh-n<u>oo</u> a dooz uh-roh. la soop doo zhoor, say kwa?
Well I'm going to have the fixed-price menu, at 12 euros. What's the soup of the day?

Serveur **Une bisque de homard, ou bien une vichyssoise**
<u>oo</u>n beesk de o-mar, oo byañ <u>oo</u>n vee-shee-swaz
Lobster soup, or vichyssoise (cold leek and potato soup)

Alain   **Ah mais moi, je suis allergique aux fruits de mer,**
         donc je vais prendre la vichyssoise
         a may mwa zhuh sweez a-ler-zheek oh frwee duh mehr,
         doñk zhuh vay proñdr la vee-shee-swaz
         I'm allergic to seafood, so I'll have the vichyssoise

Serveur **Très bien. Et comme boisson?**
         tray byañ. ay kom bwa-soñ?
         Very good. And to drink?

Alain   **Un pichet de vin rouge, et une bouteille d'eau,**
         s'il vous plaît
         uñ pee-shay duh vañ roozh, ay oon boo-tay doh,
         seel voo play
         A jug of red wine and a bottle of water, please

         (at the end of the meal)

Alain   **Monsieur!**
         muhss-yuh!
         Excuse me!

Serveur **Vous avez terminé?**
         vooz a-vay tehr-mee-nay?
         Have you finished?

Delphine **Oui, merci. C'était très bon**
         wee mehr-see. say-tay tray boñ
         Yes, thanks. It was very good

Alain   **Est-ce qu'on peut avoir l'addition, s'il vous plaît?**
         ess koñ puh a-vwar la-deess-yoñ, seel voo play?
         Could we have the bill, please?

Serveur **Oui, bien sûr, je vous l'apporte tout de suite**
         wee, byañ soor, zhuh voo la-port toot sweet
         Yes, of course, I'll bring it straight away

Alain   **Vous prenez les cartes bleues?**
         voo pruh-nay lay kart bluh?
         Do you take credit cards?

Serveur **Oui monsieur, sans problème**
         wee muhss-yuh, soñ prob-lem
         Yes sir, no problem

installez-vous
añ-sta-lay voo
take a seat

vous avez choisi?
vooz a-vay shwa-zee?
have you chosen?

pas encore
pa oñ-kor
not yet

je suis végétarien(ne)
zhuh swee vay-zhay-tar-yañ(yen)
I'm a vegetarian

je vais prendre …
zhuh vay proñdr …
I'll have …

je suis allergique aux
œufs
zhuh sweez a-lehr-zheek ohz uh
I'm allergic to eggs

c'était très bon
say-tay tray boñ
it was very good

tout de suite
toot sweet
straight away

sans problème
soñ prob-lem
no problem

À la carte

Yes, the word menu exists in French, but be careful, it doesn't refer to the card the choices are printed on! It means the options themselves, as in a fixed-price 'set menu'. What the waiter hands to you to look at is la carte (literally 'the card') – which is the origin of that old-fashioned concept of dining 'à la carte', choosing freely from the menu rather than being restricted to a fixed set of choices.

C'est ça!
A useful way of confirming what someone has said, or encouraging them when they're doing something right. Literally, 'it's that', ie 'that's right'.

You asked a question, didn't you?
Notice how often a question is made by simply recycling a statement. It's almost as if you make the assertion then challenge the other person to contradict you: 'that's right, isn't it?', 'you've chosen, have you?', 'you accept credit cards, I suppose?' Here are some examples, with the alternative question forms in brackets:
c'est bien ça? (est-ce que c'est bien ça? est-ce bien ça?) 'is that right?'
vous avez choisi? (est-ce que vous avez choisi? avez-vous choisi?) 'have you chosen?'
vous prenez les cartes bleues? (est-ce que vous prenez les cartes bleues? prenez-vous les cartes bleues?) 'do you take credit cards?'
This little trick really makes your life easier as a learner!

Quelle surprise!
When you see the phrase quels plats? 'what/which dishes?' you may already be guessing that the -s of quels is there because plats is plural. French doesn't make the distinction we have between 'which' and 'what', but quel works according to a pattern you may be starting to recognise: quel/quelle/quels/quelles. 'Which dish' would have been quel plat, and if the word in question was feminine, an extra -le would be needed: quelle adresse? 'which address?', quelles langues parlez-vous? 'what languages do you speak?' > Questions RefZone 15.

Straight talking
Installez-vous 'sit down, take a seat' the waiter tells his customers simply. Often in French it's possible to give a straightforward command in a perfectly polite way, where we mealy-mouthed English speakers might feel the need to add a please or a question to soften the impact: 'Do sit down! Please take a seat! If you wouldn't mind signing here ... ' and so on.

did you know ...?

A different type of carte
If you've been to France you'll have seen the logo CB in all sorts of places. The Carte Bleue is the best-known credit card in France, and is just used to mean credit cards in general, like saying 'Hoover' for vacuum cleaner.

Comme again?

Comme is one of the most useful words you'll learn. Generally speaking it means 'as', but here it's something like 'by way of', and it can help simplify the job of asking questions – et comme boisson? – something like 'and by way of a drink?', or in other words 'what kind of drink would you like?' Comme plat principal vous pouvez prendre ... 'For your main dish you can have ...'. Suppose you want to ask in a shop about their range of hats. You could ask quelles sortes de chapeaux avez-vous?, or you could just say simply 'what have you got in the way of hats?': qu'est-ce que vous avez comme chapeaux?

All well and good

It's easy to get confused between bon and bien. The first is an adjective, something that describes a noun, so it's equivalent to 'good'; the second is an adverb, so it normally goes with a verb, like English 'well'. C'était très bon 'it (the food) was very good'. Comment allez-vous? Bien merci. 'How are you? I'm well, thanks.' Nowadays some people say 'I'm good' instead of 'I'm well', but if you said in French je suis bon(ne) that would mean you were good at something. Je ne suis pas très bonne, says Amandine, 'I'm not very good (at English)'; je ne parle pas très bien français, replies Katy, 'I don't speak French very well'.

All's well

There isn't always a clear distinction between bon and bien. For example, both can be used as exclamations showing approval: bon! bien! 'OK! good!' très bien! 'Fine!' Sometimes you don't really need an extra word in English to translate bien: amusez-vous bien! 'Have fun, have a good time!', or literally 'amuse yourselves well!' Often bien just adds a sort of reinforcing emphasis: c'est bien ça? 'is that (indeed) right?', bien sûr 'of course, certainly' (literally something like 'sure indeed'). And bien occurs in a lot of phrases where in literal terms it means little or nothing: eh bien ... 'well ...'; je veux bien, 'OK by me, I'd like that'.

extra vocabulary

to reserve a table
réserver une table
ray-zer-vay oon ta-bluh

course/dish
le plat
luh pla

starter
l'entrée
loñ-tray

main course
le plat principal
luh pla prañ-see-pal

dessert
le dessert
luh day-sehr

menu
la carte
la kart

wine list
la carte des vins
la kart day vañ

fried
frit(e)
free(t)

roasted
rôti(e)
roh-tee

grilled
grillé(e)
gree-yay

baked
au four
oh foor

steamed
à la vapeur
a la va-puhr

gluten free
sans gluten
soñ gloo-ten

now practise

17

> **bon and bien**

Shopping

get to know ...

> foodstuffs
> asking for things
> opening times
> quantities

Bruno **Tiens, voilà une épicerie! Il faut que j'achète deux ou trois bricoles**
tyañ, vwa-la oon ay-pee-suh-ree! eel foh kuh zha-shet duh oo trwa bree-kol
Hey, there's a grocers! I need to buy a couple of things

Amélie **D'accord, allons-y. Et après, on passera à la boulangerie**
da-kor, a-loñz ee. ay a-pray, oñ pass-uh-ra a la boo-loñ-zhuh-ree
Ok, let's go. And afterwards we'll go to the baker's

Vendeuse **Bonsoir messieurs dames. Vous désirez?**
boñ-swar mayss-yuh dam, voo day-zee-ray?
Good evening sir, good evening madam. What would you like?

Bruno **Bonsoir. Vous avez du jambon?**
boñ-swar. vooz a-vay doo zhoñ-boñ?
Good evening. Do you have any ham?

Vendeuse **Oui. Vous voulez du jambon blanc ou du jambon fumé?**
wee. voo voo-lay doo zhoñ-boñ bloñ oo doo zhoñ-boñ foo-may?
Yes. Do you want cooked ham or cured ham?

Bruno **Euh, je voudrais cinq tranches de jambon blanc, s'il vous plaît**
uh, zhuh voo-dray sañk troñsh duh zhoñ-boñ bloñ, seel voo play
Er, I'd like five slices of cooked ham, please

Vendeuse **Voilà. Et avec ceci?**
vwa-la. ay a-vek suh-see?
There we are. Anything else?

Bruno **Je voudrais des chips, s'il vous plaît**
zhuh voo-dray day sheeps, seel voo play
I'd like some crisps, please

Vendeuse **Elles sont là-bas, sur le rayon derrière vous. Servez-vous**
el soñ la-ba, soor luh ra-yoñ dehr-yehr voo. ser-vay voo
They're over there, on the shelf behind you. Help yourself

Amélie **Et du fromage. Vous avez de l'emmenthal?**
ay doo fro-mazh. vooz a-vay duh lem-añ-tal?
And some cheese. Do you have any emmenthal?

Vendeuse	**Oui, bien sûr. Vous en voulez combien?**
	wee, byañ soor. vooz oñ voo-lay koñb-yañ?
	Yes, certainly. How much would you like?
Amélie	**Euh ... Deux cents grammes, s'il vous plaît**
	uh ... duh soñ gram, seel voo play
	Er ... 200 grams, please
Vendeuse	**Voilà. Ce sera tout?**
	vwa-la. suh suh-ra too?
	There we are. Will that be everything?
Bruno	**Je prends un kilo de pommes, et ce sera tout.**
	Je vous dois combien?
	zhuh proñ uñ kee-lo duh pom, ay suh suh-ra too.
	zhuh voo dwa koñ-byañ?
	I'll have a kilo of apples, and that'll be everything.
	How much do I owe you?
Vendeuse	**Alors, en tout, ça fait neuf euros quarante-cinq**
	a-lor, oñ too, sa fay nuhf uh-roh ka-roñt-sañk
	Well, that makes 9 euros 45 in total
Bruno	**Voilà. Je vous remercie!**
	vwa-la. zhuh voo ruh-mehr-see!
	There we are. Thanks very much!
Vendeuse	**C'est moi qui vous remercie. Au revoir,**
	messieurs dames!
	say mwa kee voo ruh-mehr-see. oh ruh-vwar,
	mayss-yuh dam!
	Thank you. Goodbye!

from the dialogue

il faut que j'achète ...
eel foh kuh zha-shet ...
I need to buy ...

allons-y
a-loñz-ee
let's go

cinq tranches de ...
sañk troñsh duh ...
five slices of ...

sur le rayon
soor luh ra-yon
on the shelf

servez-vous
ser-vay voo
help yourselves

du fromage
doo fro-mazh
some cheese

vous en voulez combien?
vooz oñ voo-lay koñ-byañ?
how much do you want?

je vous dois combien?
zhuh voo dwa koñ-byañ?
how much do I owe you?

ça fait ...
sa fay ...
that comes to ...

en tout
oñ too
in total

Ladies and gents

As we've seen, you may well be addressed as monsieur, madame or maybe, if young, mademoiselle, by people working in shops or elsewhere. If you're in a couple or a group, here are the plurals: monsieur–messieurs, madame–mesdames, mademoiselle–mesdemoiselles. But what if you are in a mixed group? That's when you end up with the phrase messieurs dames – sort of 'sir(s) and madam(s)'!

18

Tell me your deepest desires

A common way of asking someone what they want is to use a kind of unfinished statement vous désirez? 'what would you like?' It's as if you're leaving the other person to complete the sentence for you: 'You'd like … ?' The answer doesn't usually involve the verb désirer, though: just say je voudrais … (the conditional tense of vouloir, 'to want'), 'I'd like … '.

Self-service

The verb servir crops up a lot in shop situations, and also at mealtimes. The French use it more often than we would say 'to serve'. Qu'est-ce que je vous sers? is literally 'what do I serve you?' And for 'help yourself' we have the phrase servez-vous 'serve yourself'.

Pièce de résistance

The French word pièce has various important meanings, more than one of which you will encounter on shopping trips. Pièce can mean 'coin', short for pièce d'argent, but you can see it on signs meaning 'unit', eg choux-fleurs 1€ pièce 'cauliflowers €1 each'. It also means a room, or a play (une pièce de théâtre), and you may well be asked for une pièce d'identité (a document constituting proof of ID). Another example of a word with many important meanings is carte: card, map, menu, etc. A good dictionary is what you need to keep track of these.

Chips with everything

Don't get confused over your snack foods! In French, following American English, les chips are potato crisps (pronounced sheeps). Chips in the sense of French fries are les frites.

Thanking you

You will often hear the phrase je vous remercie 'I thank you' as a more polite variant of merci. A shopkeeper will sometimes reply, c'est moi qui vous remercie 'it's me who is thanking you', or 'thank *you*' as we would say.

> ### did you know …?
>
> The French use the 24-hour clock more widely than we do, so you will typically see things like '9h–14h' (9am–2pm).
> > h – heures (20h = 8pm)
> > Ouverture – opening
> > Heures d'ouverture – opening hours
> > Jours fériés – public holidays
> > Jours de congé – holidays, days off
> > Jours ouvrables – working days
> > Heures ouvrables – business hours
> > Vacances – holidays

Euro pound

Une livre means a pound, in weight or money, but not necessarily the Imperial one we know in Britain. In France it is used to refer to the 'metric pound' of 500g. It's used especially by older people – just like imperial measures in Britain.

On the shelf

In English we refer to the aisle or section where something is to be found; in French you usually specify the shelf (le rayon). You don't need a de or anything in this case, it's just le rayon ... followed directly by the name of the thing you want: le rayon pâtisserie the baking aisle, le rayon vins the wine department. This is especially useful in department stores, les grands magasins or supermarkets, les grandes surfaces.

extra vocabulary

large
grand(e)
groñ(d)

medium
moyen(-enne)
mwa-yañ/mwa-yen

small
petit(e)
puh-tee(t)

a piece of ...
une morceau de ...
uñ mor-soh duh ...

a kilo of ...
un kilo de ...
uñ kee-loh duh ...

a pound (500g) of ...
une livre de ...
oon leev-ruh duh ...

a packet of ...
un paquet de ...
uñ pa-kay duh ...

a tin of ...
une boîte de ...
oon bwat duh ...

Hamming it up

In France ham can be cooked (the usual sort in the UK, known in French as jambon cuit, jambon de Paris or jambon d'York), or cured, that is, air-dried (jambon cru, literally 'raw ham'). The latter is not to everyone's taste so make sure you know what you're getting!

now practise

(19)

> shopping

Buying shoes

get to know ...

> sizes
> colours
> none, nothing, no longer

Vendeuse **Bonjour madame, je peux vous aider?**
boñ-zhoor ma-dam, zhuh puh vooz ay-day?
Good morning, can I help you?

Louise **Je voudrais essayer ces chaussures en noir, s'il vous plaît**
zhuh voo-dray e-say-yay say shoh-soor oñ nwar, seel voo play
I'd like to try these shoes in black, please

Vendeuse **Vous faites quelle pointure?**
voo fet kel pwañ-toor?
What size are you?

Louise **Je fais du trente-neuf**
zhuh fay doo troñt-nuhf
I'm a size 39

Vendeuse **Je vais les chercher. Je reviens tout de suite**
zhuh vay lay shehr-shay. zhuh ruh-vyañ toot sweet
I'll go and get them. I'll be right back

Vendeuse **Voilà le trente-neuf**
vwa-la luh troñt-nuhf
Here's the 39

Louise **C'est dommage, elles sont trop petites. Vous les avez en plus grand?**
say do-mazh, el soñ troh puh-teet. voo layz a-vay oñ ploo groñ?
What a pity, they are too small. Do you have them in a bigger size?

Vendeuse **Je vais voir si je les ai en quarante**
zhuh vay vwar see zhuh layz ay oñ ka-roñt
I'll go and see if we have them in 40

Vendeuse **Voilà le quarante. Vous voulez les essayer?**
vwa-la luh ka-roñt. voo voo-lay layz e-say-yay?
Here is size 40. Would you like to try them on?

Louise Oui ... elles vont très bien, merci. Je les prends
wee ... el voñ tray byañ, mehr-see. zhuh lay proñ
Yes ... they fit very well, thanks. I'll take them

Vendeuse Très bien! Vous payez à la caisse, madame
tray byañ. voo pa-yay a la kess, ma-dam
Very good. Please pay at the cash desk, madam

I'll take them

In French the present tense is often used to express an intention or an offer, where the future would be used in English. In shops and cafés you are often asked qu'est-ce que je vous sers? 'what shall I get you? what would you like?', literally 'what do I serve you?' je prends une bière 'I'll have a beer'. This phrase je prends ... 'I'll have, I'll take, I'd like', literally 'I take' is very useful for ordering things and specifying choices.

Size is important

There are different words in French for sizes of different items of clothing. The basic word for size is la taille, and this works for dresses, skirts, jackets, trousers and so on; for shirts, you traditionally specify the collar size (encolure), and with shoes, it's la pointure. Also remember to use the verb faire where English would say 'take': vous faites quelle pointure? 'what size do you take?'; je fais du trente-neuf 'I'm a size 39'. Of course if buying clothes in Europe you will need to know what you take in continental sizes!

from the dialogue

je voudrais essayer ...
zhuh voo-dray e-say-yay ...
I'd like to try ...

ces chaussures
say shoh-soor
these shoes

en noir
oñ nwar
in black

vous faites quelle pointure?
voo fet kel pwañ-toor?
what size are you?

je fais du trente-neuf
zhuh fay doo troñt-nuhf
I take a size 39

c'est dommage
say do-mazh
what a pity

trop petit(e)s
troh puh-tee(t)
too small

en plus grand
oñ ploo groñ
in a bigger size

je les prends
zhuh lay proñ
I'll take them

à la caisse
a la kess
at the cash desk

SOLDES
TOUT DOIT
DISPARAITRE
SOLDES

Comparatively comfortable

The shoes are 'too small' – trop petites – and so a bigger pair is needed. This is a case where French is more straightforward than English, where some words take the '-er' ending ('small – smaller') and others use the word 'more' ('comfortable – more comfortable'). This is known as the comparative. In the next dialogue we'll see how to make the superlative, as in 'smallest', or 'most comfortable'.

Women's clothes sizes

UK/Australia	8	10	12	14	16	18	20	22
Europe	36	38	40	42	44	46	48	50
US/Canada	6	8	10	12	14	16	18	20

Men's clothes sizes (suits)

UK/US/Canada	36	38	40	42	44	46
Europe	46	48	50	52	54	56
Austrailia	92	97	102	107	112	117

Shoes

UK/Australia	2	3	4	5	6	7	8	9	10	11
Europe	35	36	37	38	39	41	42	43	45	46
US/Canada women	4	5	6	7	8	9	10	11	12	-
US/Canada men	3	4	5	6	7	8	9	10	11	12

Children's shoes

UK/US/Canada	0	1	2	3	4	5	6	7	8	9	10	11
Europe	15	17	18	19	20	22	23	24	26	27	28	29

Please please me

As well as aimer, you can use the verb plaire to describe your likes and dislikes. J'aime la natation 'I like swimming' would then become la natation me plaît, literally 'swimming pleases me'. Of course that sounds very old-fashioned in English, but not in French. It's what's behind the expression s'il vous plaît, literally 'if it pleases you'.

No way, never, no more

Negatives, as we know, are constructed using the two words ne and pas – although you're allowed to drop the ne in informal speech. L'autre paire ne vous plaît pas? 'You don't like the other pair?' Now let's meet some other negative constructions with ne. To say that something is no longer the case, use ne ... plus; to say that something is never true, use ne ... jamais. And for 'nobody, no-one', we use ne ... personne. For example: Je n'ai plus ces chaussures 'I no longer have those shoes, I haven't got those shoes any more'. Je ne vais jamais en vacances 'I never go on holiday'. Il n'y a personne au bureau 'there's nobody at the office'. Again, you'll find the ne being dropped in these cases, in informal speech. > NEGATIVES REFZONE 16.

Shades of meaning

When asking what colour something is, you say de quelle couleur est-il? (or est-elle if the thing is feminine) – literally 'of what colour is it?' Colours are adjectives. For light colours, you use the word clair, and for dark colours foncé: bleu clair/rouge foncé 'light blue/dark red'.

> COLOURS REFZONE 13.

Cherry red and apple blossom

Because colours are adjectives, they agree with the noun they describe – des pommes vertes 'some green apples'. The colour always goes after the noun it describes. Some colours, ones that come from the name of fruit and nuts (eg orange and marron 'chestnut', used for 'brown') never change; so brown shoes would be des chaussures marron.

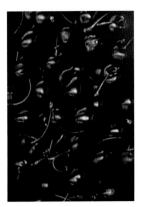

At the station

get to know ...

> superlatives
> writing figures
> which one?
> times

Anna   **Bonjour monsieur. Il est à quelle heure, le prochain train pour Nice?**
boñ-zhoor muhss-yuh. eel ayt a kel uhr luh pro-shañ trañ poor neess?
Hello. What time is the next train to Nice, please?

Assistant   **Il y a un TGV à onze heures huit (11h08) qui arrive à Nice à seize heures trois (16h03). Vous voulez un aller simple ou un aller-retour?**
eel ee a uñ tay-zhay-vay a oñz uhr weet kee a-reev a neess a sehz uhr trwa. voo voo-lay uññ a-lay sañpl ou uññ a-lay-ruh-toor?
There's a TGV at 11.08am which arrives at Nice at 4.03pm. Do you want a single or a return?

Anna   **Un aller simple, c'est combien?**
uññ a-lay sañpl, say koñb-yañ?
How much is a single?

Assistant   **Avez-vous une carte de réduction?**
a-vay voo oon kart duh ray-dooks-yoñ?
Are you entitled to any reductions?

Anna   **Oui, j'ai la carte Senior**
wee, zhay la kart sen-yor
Yes, I have a senior citizen's card

Assistant   **Alors vous avez droit à cinquante pour cent (50 %) de réduction. Ça vous fait donc trente-cinq euros trente (35,30 €) y compris la réservation qui est obligatoire pour les TGV**
a-lor vooz a-vay drwa a sañ-koñt poor-soñ duh ray-dooks-yoñ. sa voo fay doñk troñt sañk uh-roh troñt ee koñ-pree la ray-zehr-vass-yoñ kee ayt o-blee-ga-twar poor lay tay-zhay-vay
Then you are entitled to a 50% reduction. That makes it €35.30 including the reservation which is obligatory on TGVs

Anna   **C'est parfait. Et le TGV part de quel quai?**
say par-fay. ay luh tay-zhay-vay par duh kel kay?
That's perfect. And which platform does the TGV leave from?

Assistant **Du quai numéro deux. Voilà votre billet. Vous avez la place numéro quarante-cinq dans la voiture sept. Bon voyage!**

doo kay noo-may-ro duh. vwa-la vo-truh bee-yay. vooz a-vay la plass noo-may-roh ka-roñt sañk doñ la vwa-toor set. boñ vwa-yazh!

From platform 2. Here is your ticket. You're in seat number 45, coach 7. Have a good trip!

(on the platform)

Anna **Pardon monsieur, le train pour Nice, c'est lequel? C'est celui-ci?**

par-doñ muhss-yuh, luh trañ poor neess, say luh-kel? say suhl-wee see?

Excuse me, which is the train for Nice? Is it this one?

Porteur **Non, ce n'est pas celui-là. Le train pour Nice est en retard, il n'est pas encore arrivé en gare**

noñ, suh nay pa suh-lwee-la. luh trañ poor neess ayt oñ ruh-tar, eel nay paz oñ-kor a-ree-vay oñ gar

No, it's not that one. The Nice train is late, it hasn't arrived in the station yet

Anna **Mais c'est bien ce quai-ci?**

may say byañ suh kay see?

But it is indeed this platform?

Porteur **Non madame, c'est ce quai-là pour Nice**

noñ ma-dam, say suh kay-la poor neess

No madam, it's that platform there for Nice

Anna **Lequel?**

luh-kel?

Which one?

Porteur **Celui-là, le deux**

suhl-wee-la, luh duh

That one, number 2

did you know ...?

The railways in France are a source of great national pride, and the famous TGV *tay-zhay-vay*, or train à grande vitesse 'high-speed train', is the flagship of the fleet. It runs fast and smooth on specially constructed tracks. Naturally it's more expensive than ordinary trains like the TER (train express régional, 'regional express train') and reservation is obligatory. To find out more about trains in France visit www.sncf.com.

Cheap as chips

The French translation usually given for 'cheap' is bon marché. But in practice it's very common to use the word cher 'expensive' in negative constructions. So 'cheaper' is very often moins cher 'less expensive'. When it comes to discounts, you typically specify such-and-such a percentage of reduction: cinquante pourcent de réduction 'a 50% reduction'.

Superlative stuff

In English we have two ways of comparing one thing to another or to all the rest: -er and -est (cheap – cheaper – cheapest), and the words 'more' and 'most' (economical – more economical – most economical). In French you use the word plus for both: une voiture plus économique 'a more economical car', and la voiture la plus économique 'the most economical car'. This applies to adverbs as well as adjectives: ce train va plus vite this train goes faster; c'est plus long 'it's longer'. In the case of things that are less, or the least, you use moins. As explained above, it is also the word often used to translate 'cheap': moins cher 'less expensive' le/la moins cher 'the least expensive'.

There is or there are?

In French you don't need to worry whether 'there is' one thing or 'there are' several. The phrase that pays is il y a and it covers both singular and plural: il y a un train 'there is a train', il y a des tarifs différents 'there are different prices (rates)'.

Well, well

As we've seen, one of the many uses of the word bien is to confirm or strengthen something: C'est bien l'arrêt de bus pour ..., 'is this (indeed) the right bus for ... ' J'aime bien ce modèle 'I (do) like this style.' Another example is the expression je veux bien. It's a very common way of agreeing to things, meaning something like 'yes, I'd like that, that's fine by me'. Often where in English we would say 'yes please', the authentic expression in French, rather than oui s'il vous plaît, would be simply je veux bien.

Time and money

We've shown in brackets how times and sums of money are written out. The times are of course specified in the 24-hour clock, with the letter 'h' to separate hours and minutes, so that 18h35 is 6.35pm, and for money the euro symbol (and indeed the pound symbol when the French write it) tends to come after the amount rather than before: 35,30 €. One more thing to watch out for: the full stop and the comma are used the other way around in French, with the full stop separating thousands, and the decimals coming after a comma: €6,999.95 is 6.999,95 €.

This one, that one

We've seen how to say 'this (thing) here' and 'that (thing) there', but what if you just want to say 'this one' or 'that one'? You need the word celui (celle for the feminine, ceux/celles for masculine/feminine plural). So you could find ce train-ci? – oui, celui-là 'this train? – yes, that one' or cette porte-là? non, celle-ci 'that door? – no, this one'. To ask the question 'which one?' you need the word lequel (laquelle for feminine singular, lesquels/lequelles for masculine/feminine plural). > DEMONSTRATIVES REFZONE 12.

> DEMONSTRATIVES REFZONE 12.

---

extra vocabulary

the train leaves ...
le train part ...
luh trañ par ...

the film starts ...
le film commence ...
luh feelm ko-moñss ...

at one o'clock
à une heure
a oon uhr

at two thirty
à deux heures et demie
a duhz uhr ay duh-mee

at 1600 hours
à seize heures
a sez uhr

at five to five
à cinq heures moins cinq
a sañk uhr mwañ sañk

at a quarter to six
à six heures moins le quart
a seez uhr mwañ luh kar

at twenty-five to seven
à sept heures moins vingt-cinq
a set uhr mwañ vañt-sañk

at midnight
à minuit
a meen-wee

at midday
à midi
a mee-dee

at 22.48
à vingt-deux heures quarante-huit
a vañ-duhz uhr ka-roñt weet

---

now practise

> **understanding railway announcements**

Catching a bus

get to know ...

> ago
> savoir and connaître
> avoir and être verbs
> buses

Caroline **Excusez-moi, madame! C'est bien l'arrêt de bus pour aller en ville?**
eks-koo-zay-mwa, ma-dam! say byañ la-ray duh boos poor a-lay oñ veel?
Excuse me! Is this the right stop for the bus into town?

Mme Brun **Oui, c'est ça. Vous pouvez prendre le bus numéro quinze**
wee, say sa. voo poo-vay proñdr luh boos noo-may-roh kañz
Yes, that's right. You can get the number 15 bus

Caroline **Et le bus passe souvent?**
ay luh boos pass soo-voñ?
And does the bus go often?

Mme Brun **Oui, il passe toutes les dix minutes. Le dernier est passé il y a cinq minutes**
wee, eel pass toot lay dee mee-noot. luh dern-yay ay pass-ay eel ee a sañk mee-noot
Yes, it goes every 10 minutes. The last one went by five minutes ago

Caroline **Et on peut acheter des tickets au conducteur?**
ay oñ puh ash-tay day tee-kay oh koñ-dook-tuhr?
Can I buy tickets from the driver?

Mme Brun **Oui, sans problème. Tenez, voilà le quinze qui arrive! Allez-y, montez!**
wee, soñ prob-lehm. tuh-nay, vwa-la luh kañz kee a-reev! a-layz-ee, moñ-tay!
Yes, no problem. Hey, there's the number 15 coming! Go ahead, get on!

(on board)

Caroline **Bonjour monsieur. Un ticket, s'il vous plaît**
boñ-zhoor muhss-yuh. uñ tee-kay, seel voo play
Good morning. A ticket, please

Conducteur **Un euro vingt (1,20 €)**
uñn uh-roh vañ
One euro 20

Caroline **Vous passez devant l'office de tourisme?**
voo pa-say duh-voñ lo-feess duh too-reezm?
Do you go past the tourist office?

Conducteur **Oui, descendez à l'arrêt juste avant la gare**
wee, day-soñ-day a la-reh zhoost a-voñ la gar
Yes, get off at the stop just before the station

Caroline **Vous pourrez me dire quand descendre? Je ne connais pas bien la ville**
voo poo-ray muh deer koñ day-soñdr? zhuh nuh kon-nay pa byañ la veel
Could you tell me when to get off? I don't know the town very well

Conducteur **D'accord. Asseyez-vous à l'avant, et je vous dirai où descendre**
da-kor. a-say-yay voo a la-voñ, ay zhuh voo dee-ray oo day-soñdr
OK. Sit at the front and I will tell you when to get off

Caroline **Merci!**
mehr-see!
Thanks!

Once upon a time

The word 'ago' is fairly straightforward to turn into French. It's that very useful little phrase il y a again. We've already seen that this means 'there is' or 'there are', but it also places events in the past: il y a cinq minutes 'five minutes ago'.

Knowing me, knowing you

If you know that savoir means 'to know', you may be wondering why it's je ne connais pas bien la ville 'I don't know the town very well' rather than 'je ne sais pas bien la ville'. In fact there are two different kinds of knowing: you can be familiar with something, like a person or a place 'I know John well', 'I don't know the town well', or you can be aware of something, like a fact 'I know John is busy', 'I didn't know Manchester was so big'. For the first sort there is connaître, for the second savoir.

from the dialogue

c'est bien l'arrêt de bus pour ... ?
say byañ la-ray duh boos poor ... ?
is this the right bus stop for ... ?

vous pouvez prendre ...
voo poo-vay proñdr ...
you can get ...

le bus passe souvent?
luh boos pass soo-voñ?
does the bus go often?

toutes les dix minutes
toot lay dee mee-noot
every ten minutes

il y a cinq minutes
eel ee a sañk mee-noot
five minutes ago

on peut acheter ...
oñ puh ash-tay ...
you can buy ...

allez-y, montez!
a-layz-ee, moñ-tay!
go ahead, get on!

je ne connais pas bien la ville
zhuh nuh kon-nay pa byañ la veel
I don't know the town very well

Minding your à and le

On peut acheter des tickets au conducteur? 'Can one buy tickets from the driver?' Notice that the word à (in the contracted form au because of the masculine noun that follows: à+le=au) is used here, rather than de (or rather du, from de+le) as you might expect given that it's so often the translation of English 'from'.

On and off, up and down

In French you 'get up into' (monter dans) and 'get down from' (descendre de) the bus, much as in English where we get 'on' and 'off'. Same for trains and planes – and automobiles too. Where in English we get 'in' and 'out' of the car, in French you monter dans la voiture or 'get up into' it, and descendre (get down) at the end. A relic of the early days of motoring where some real climbing up and down was required!

At the front, at the back

More vehicle vocab: 'at the front' is à l'avant, while 'at the back' is, logically enough à l'arrière.

Bus passes

The bus 'goes' or 'runs' every so often in English. But in French it 'passes': Le bus passe souvent? 'does the bus go often?' Oui, il passe toutes les dix minutes 'yes, it goes every ten minutes'. And whereas buses passent in French, trains circulent. So on train timetables you see jours de circulation meaning 'days of operation'.

did you know ...?

Just the ticket

You may know the French word billet for 'ticket'. That is indeed the right word for trains and air travel, among other uses. But on buses, it's called a ticket (pronounced *tee-kay*). Incidentally if you're going to be travelling around by bus or Metro you can save money by buying a book of 10 tickets, called a carnet.

In French cities, night buses Noctambus – a pun on noctambule meaning 'night owl' – operate seven days a week from 1am to 5.30am. You pay a fixed fare for the journey. Look out for the Noctambus sign at the bus stop to check if it stops.

To have or to be

Most verbs can be put into the past using the verb avoir, 'to have' just as English uses 'to have' in 'I have done it', for example j'ai acheté des cartes postales 'I've bought (or 'I bought') some postcards'. However, a few very common verbs use être, 'to be'. One of them is passer when it means to go past: Le dernier est passé il y a cinq minutes 'the last one went by five minutes ago'. Other verbs in this category are: aller 'to go', venir 'to come', entrer 'to come/go in', sortir 'to come/go out', arriver 'to arrive', partir 'to leave', revenir 'to come back', retourner 'to go back', rentrer 'to return', monter 'to come/go up', descendre 'to come/go down', tomber 'to fall', rester 'to stay', devenir 'to become', naître 'to be born', mourir 'to die'.

the bus station
la gare routière
la gar root-yehr

a bus stop
un arrêt de bus
uñn a-ray duh-boos

bus number 9
le bus numéro neuf
luh boos noo-may-roh nuhf

to catch the bus
prendre le bus
proñdr luh boos

to get on the bus
monter dans le bus
moñ-tay doñ luh boos

to get off the bus
descendre du bus
day-soñ-druh doo boos

do you go to the station?
vous allez à la gare?
vooz a-lay a la gar?

the coach
le car
luh kar

how long does it take?
combien de temps faut-il?
koñb-yañ duh toñ foht-eel?

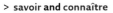

> savoir and connaître

25

An internet café

get to know ...

> il faut que ...
> web addresses
> emphatic pronouns
> internet vocabulary

Amélie **Louise, tu sais où il y a un cybercafé dans ton quartier? Il faut que je confirme par courriel pour la réunion de la semaine prochaine**
loo-eez, too say oo eel ee a uñ see-ber-ka-fay doñ toñ kar-tee-ay? eel foh kuh zhuh koñ-feerm par koor-yel poor la ray-oo-nee-oñ de la suh-men pro-shen
Louise, do you know where there is an internet cafe in your part of town? I need to confirm by email next week's meeting

Louise **Oui, pas de problème, il y en a un au coin de la rue. Je t'y emmène**
wee, pa duh prob-lehm, eel ee oñn a uñ oh kwañ duh la roo. zhuh tee oñ-men
Yes, no problem. There is one at the corner of the street. I'll take you there

Amélie **Tu sais combien ça coûte pour se connecter?**
too say koñ-byañ sa koot poor suh ko-nek-tay?
Do you know how much it costs to go online?

Louise **Je crois que c'est 3 euros de l'heure. Tiens, au fait, je n'ai pas ton email. Tu peux me le donner?**
zhuh krwa kuh say trwaz uh-roh duh luhr. tyañ, oh fet, zhuh nay pa toñn ee-mel. too puh muh luh do-nay?
I think it's 3 euros per hour. Hey, by the way, I don't have your e-mail address. Can you give it to me?

Amélie **Oui, c'est (amelie76@cybermel.fr) amelie soixante-seize arobase cybermel point f r. Et toi, quel est ton email?**
wee, sayt am-ay-lee swa-soñt-sehz a-ro-baz see-ber-mel pwañ eff er. ay twa, kel ay toñn ee-mel?
Yes, it's amelie seventy-six at cybermel dot f r. And you, what's your e-mail address?

Louise **Moi, c'est l point karim arobase sagelor point f r (l.karim@sagelor.fr). C'est mon adresse au bureau, je n'ai pas d'adresse personnelle. On y va?**
mwa say el pwañ ka-reem a-ro-baz sa-zhay-lor pwañ eff er. say moñn a-dress oh boo-roh, zhuh nay pa da-dress per-so-nel. oñn ee va?
Mine is l.karim@sagelor.fr. That's my work address, I don't have a personal address. Shall we go?

The French have a word for it

One of those words which doesn't have a very satisfactory English translation is quartier, as in the famous Quartier Latin or Latin Quarter. District? Neighbourhood? Barrio? They all sound a bit American to British ears.

Where it's @

E-mail addresses are international and very straightforward in writing, but you may find yourself needing to read one out, at which point you will need to know the conventional pronunciation of the various bits. That squiggle we call the 'at' sign is arobase in French, while the dot is point. Anything not recognisable as a word is spelt out, eg for www.collins.co.uk *doo-bluh-vay doo-bluh-vay doo-bluh-vay ko-leenz pwañ say oh pwañ oo ka.*

Il faut que ...

Il faut que je confirme 'I must confirm', literally 'it's necessary that I should confirm'. This is one of the commonest ways of expressing a necessity in French: il faut que followed by what's called the subjunctive, a form used to express a hypothetical reality. You don't necessarily have to have the que ... part either: il faut confirmer par mail 'it's necessary to confirm by email', il faut un ordinateur 'a computer is necessary, you need a computer'. Another way of making it personal is to slip in a me/te/vous or whatever – il me faut confirmer – which is just the same as saying il faut que je confirme, but without the subjunctive verb afterwards.

www

As in English, the French don't abbreviate in speech 'double u, double u, double u'. So while *doo-bluh-vay doo-bluh-vay doo-bluh-vay* may seem a mouthful for us, it is the same for French people having to say it in English. The Italians, meanwhile, have opted for 'voo voo voo'.

from the dialogue

par courriel
par koor-yel
by email

la semaine prochaine
la suh-men pro-shen
next week

je t'y emmène
zhuh tee oñ-men
I'll take you there

se connecter
suh ko-nek-tay
to go online

trois euros de l'heure
trwaz uh-roh duh luhr
3 euros per hour

au fait
oh fet
by the way

ton email
toñn ee-mel
your e-mail address

mon adresse personnelle
moñn a-dress per-so-nel
my personal address

on y va?
oñn ee va?
shall we go?

la réunion du mardi 17
la ray-oo-nee-oñ doo mar-dee dee-set
the meeting on Tuesday 17

au bureau
oh boo-roh
in the office

26

What about 'you'?

Notice these little words toi (you) and moi (me). Et toi, quel est ton email? What do they add to the sentence? They provide emphasis, that's right, emphasis! Contrast quel est ton email? 'what's your e-mail address?' with toi, quel est ton email? 'what's **your** e-mail address?' These 'emphatic pronouns' are also a handy way to form informal statements without much 'grammar' in them, as it were! Moi, c'est l.karim@sagelor.fr is literally 'me, it's l.karim@sagelor.fr', but it's a useful way of introducing any statement about yourself. Comment tu t'appelles? Moi, c'est Anne 'what's your name? I'm Anne'. > Pronouns RefZone 18.

Tuesday's meeting

The French use de rather more often than we would say 'of': la réunion du mardi 17/de la semaine prochaine is 'the meeting of Tuesday 17/of next week'. It's a very useful word, as we may have mentioned. You should be on the lookout for this when expressing yourself in French. For example 'the problems we had last time' could just be les problèmes de la dernière fois; 'the advice the driver gave us' would be best expressed as simply les conseils du conducteur.

Don't get tense!

You'll have noticed that Amélie's email uses the future tense: je serai présente 'I will be present'. We won't go into the formation of the future here, but you can find an explanation of the various tenses. > Verbs RefZone 19.

It'll cost you

Apart from just saying that something 'is' a certain price, you can use the verb coûter 'to cost', as used in the dialogue (tu sais combien ça coûte? 'do you know how much it costs?'), or you can say that the thing is 'at' a certain price: elle est à quarante-six euros la nuit 'it's €46 a night'.

Nouveau message

| Fichier | Edition | Affichage | Outils | **Composer** | Aide | Envoyer | ✉ |

À: p.lambotte@robert.fr	**Nouveau message**
Cc:	**Répondre**
Copie cachée:	**Répondre à tous**
Objet: réunion	**Faire suivre**
	Fichier joint

Bonjour

Hello

Je vous envoie ce message pour vous confirmer que je serai présente à la réunion du mardi 17 à 15 heures dans vos bureaux.

I'm sending this message to confirm that I will be present at the meeting on Tuesday 17 at 3pm in your offices.

Amicalement

Best regards

Amélie Voinet

extra vocabulary

to send an e-mail
envoyer un mail
oñ-vwa-yay uñ mel

to receive a fax
recevoir un fax
ruh-suh-vwar uñ faks

to scan a picture
scanner une image
ska-nay oon ee-mazh

my password
mon mot de passe
moñ moh duh pass

a search engine
un moteur de recherche
uñ mo-tuhr duh ruh-shersh

the server is down
le serveur est en panne
luh ser-vuhr ayt oñ pan

the website
le site web
luh seet web

www.collins.co.uk
www point Collins point co point uk
doob-luh-vay doob-luh-vay
doob-luh-vay pwañ ko-leenz
pwañ say oh pwañ oo ka

to text somebody
envoyer un texto à quelqu'un
oñ-vwa-yay uñ teks-to a kel-kuñ

my mobile phone
mon portable
moñ por-tabl

Booking a hotel

get to know ...

> spelling aloud
> dates
> phone numbers
> oui and si

Caroline **Allô, bonjour. Je voudrais réserver une chambre pour trois nuits, du quinze au dix-sept août**
alloh, boñ-zhoor. zhuh voo-dray ray-zer-vay oon shoñ-bruh poor trwah nwee, doo kañz oh dee-set oot
Ah, hello. I would like to book a room for 3 nights, from 15 to 17 August

Réceptioniste **Attendez, ne quittez pas ... Oui, il nous reste des chambres. Quel type de chambre voulez-vous?**
a-toñ-day, nuh kee-tay pa ... wee, eel noo rest day shoñ-bruh. kel teep duh shoñ-bruh voo-lay voo?
One moment, please hold the line ... Yes, we have some rooms left. What type of room do you want?

Caroline **Je voudrais une chambre pour deux personnes avec un grand lit, et avec une salle de bain, s'il vous plaît**
zhuh voo-dray oon shoñ-bruh poor duh pehr-son avek uñ groñ lee, ay a-vek oon sal duh bañ, seel voo play
I'd like a double room with a double bed and with a bathroom, please

Réceptioniste **Ah, je regrette, il ne me reste qu'une chambre avec douche. Elle est à quarante-six (46 €) euros la nuit**
a zhuh ruh-gret, eel nuh muh rest koon shoñ-bruh a-vek doosh. el et a ka-roñt-seez uh-roh la nwee
Ah, I'm sorry, I've only got a double room with a shower. It's 46 euros per night

Caroline **C'est bien, je la prends**
say byañ, zhuh la proñ
OK, I'll take it

Réceptioniste **Très bien. Je peux avoir votre nom et votre adresse, s'il vous plaît?**
tray byañ. zhuh puh av-war votr noñ ay votr a-dress, seel voo play?
Very good. Can I have your name and your address, please?

Caroline	**Oui, c'est Caroline Smartt. Ça s'écrit S, M, A, R, deux T. J'habite au numéro vingt, Orchard Lane, Oxford**
	wee, say ka-ro-leen smart. sa say-kree es, em, a, err, duh tay. zha-beet oh noo-may-roh vañ, orchard lane, oxford
	Yes, it's Caroline Smartt. It's spelt S, M, A, R, double T. I live at number 20, Orchard Lane, Oxford
Réceptioniste	**Très bien, merci. Pourriez-vous m'envoyer une lettre de confirmation, ainsi qu'un acompte de cinquante euros?**
	tray byañ, mehr-see. poo-ree-ay voo moñ-vwa-yay oon let-ruh duh koñ-feer-mas-yoñ, añ-see kuñn a-koñt duh sañ-koñt uh-roh?
	Very good, thanks. Could you send me a letter to confirm as well as a deposit of 50 euros?
Caroline	**Oui, je vous envoie la lettre dans la semaine. Est-ce que je peux payer l'acompte par téléphone avec ma carte bleue?**
	wee, zhuh vooz oñ-vwa la let-ruh doñ la suh-men. es-kuh zhuh puh pay-yay la-koñt par tay-lay-fon a-vek ma kart bluh?
	Yes, I'll send the letter this week. Can I pay the deposit over the phone with my credit card?
Réceptioniste	**Oui, bien sûr. Donnez moi votre numéro de carte, ainsi que sa date d'expiration**
	wee, byañ soor. do-nay mwa vo-truh noo-may-ro duh kart, añ-see kuh sa dat dex-pee-rass-yoñ
	Yes, of course. Give me your card number, and its expiry date

réserver une chambre
ray-zer-vay oon shoñ-bruh
to book a room

attendez
a-toñ-day
one moment

ne quittez pas
nuh kee-tay pa
please hold the line

il nous reste ...
eel noo rest ...
we've still got ...

je regrette
zhuh ruh-gret
I'm sorry

votre nom
votr noñ
your name

votre adresse
votr a-dress
your address

ça s'écrit ...
sa say-kree ...
it's spelt ...

une lettre de confirmation
oon let-ruh duh koñ-feer-mass-yoñ
a confirmation letter

un acompte
uñn a-koñt
a deposit

dans la semaine
doñ la suh-men
within the week

au mois prochain!
oh mwa pro-shañ!
see you next month!

Spelling it out

When giving or receiving unfamiliar names verbally, you will naturally want to spell them out. Use the verb écrire, 'to write': ça s'écrit ... 'it's written ... '. For the double letters, you just say 'two': S, M, A, R, deux T – Smartt.

The dating game

Another little stress-saver: dates are given without the 'th' part in French, so not the sixteenth (of) September but the sixteen September, or as here du quinze au dix-sept août from the 15th to the 17th of August. Sometimes things are simpler in the foreign language!

Got your number

It's useful to know how to read out a phone number so as to make it understandable in French. The French tend to give long numbers as if they were real figures or amounts, so '78000' is read out as 'seventy-eight thousand' rather than 'seven eight treble zero'. Phone numbers are broken down into pairs of digits, and are usually written as such, sometimes with dots to separate the pairs, eg 01.40.20.50.50. In the case of uneven numbers of digits, you should start with the single digit, so that 01248 882030 would be zero, twelve, forty-eight, eighty-eight, twenty, thirty. > Numbers RefZone 2.

Bringing out his feminine side

Note that even if it was a man booking a room for himself, the word for 'person' is still feminine: une chambre pour une personne. Some words are always feminine, even when they refer to a man. This is because gender (whether a noun is grammatically masculine or feminine) is not the same as sex (whether a person or animal is biologically male or female). Other examples include la victime 'victim' and la vedette 'star'. Naturally, any adjective will be in the feminine in such cases: Richard Gere est une grande vedette 'Richard Gere is a great star'.

Leftovers and all the rest

When saying that you still have something, you say that it remains to you: il nous reste des chambres 'we've got some rooms left, we've still got some rooms', il ne me reste que … 'I've only got … left' – using that 'ne … que = 'only' construction. Don't forget that rester does not mean 'to rest' (which would be se reposer), it means 'to stay', in the sense of 'remain'.

Yes and no

Occasionally the French for 'yes' is not oui! When you're contradicting a negative statement, as opposed to agreeing with a positive one, you use si instead. For example if Caroline had asked 'Vous n'avez pas de chambres avec baignoire?' ('you haven't got any rooms with a bath?') the answer would have been 'Si, mais elles sont toutes prises' ('yes, but they're all taken'). Luckily, no means no, whether you're agreeing or disagreeing with someone. So: Vous avez des chambres? Oui/non. 'Have you got any rooms? Yes/no' – but: Vous n'avez pas de chambres? Si/non. 'Haven't you got any rooms? Yes/no'

did you know …?

The end

You'll notice if you read any formal letters in French that the signoff is much more verbose and formal than the English 'Yours faithfully/ sincerely'. You'll see long phrases like Je vous prie d'agréer, Monsieur, l'expression de mes sentiments les meilleurs and so on – there are dozens of possible variations, but if you need to you can probably get away with using the less formal all-purpose signoff cordialement used in the letter.

Allô allô allô

Notice that Caroline uses allô when she is on the phone. This is the greeting you generally use rather than bonjour, especially when answering the phone.

Writing to confirm

> Caroline Smartt
> 20 Orchard Lane
> Oxford OX1 3PN
>
> M Perret
> Hôtel du Lion d'Or
> 4, rue Saint-Thomas
> 14290 ORBEC
>
> Oxford, le 3 juillet 2005
> Oxford, 3 July 2005
>
> Monsieur,
> Dear Sir,
>
> Suite à notre conversation téléphonique, je vous écris afin de confirmer ma réservation dans votre hôtel d'une chambre pour deux personnes avec salle de bains, pour les trois nuits du 15 au 17 août.
> Further to our telephone conversation, I am writing to confirm my reservation at your hotel for a double room, with bathroom, for the three nights from 15 to 17 August.
>
> Cordialement,
> Yours,
>
> Caroline Smartt

now practise

> spelling aloud

a single room
une chambre pour une personne
oon shoñ-bruh poor oon pehr-son

a double room
une chambre pour deux personnes
oon shoñ-bruh poor duh pehr-son

a room for three
une chambre pour trois personnes
oon shoñ-bruh poor trwa pehr-son

a family room
une chambre familiale
oon shoñ-bruh fa-mee-lee-al

with double bed
avec un grand lit
a-vek uñ groñ lee

with twin beds
avec deux lits
a-vek duh lee

with bunk beds
avec des lits superposés
a-vek day lee soo-per-po-zay

a cot
un lit d'enfant
uñ lee doñ-foñ

for one night
pour une nuit
poor oon nwee

from 4 to 8 July
du quatre au huit juillet
doo katr oh wee zhwee-ay

for Friday night
pour la nuit de vendredi
poor la nwee duh voñ-druh-dee

Not feeling well

---

get to know ...

> illness
> reflexive verbs
> chez

Alain **Allô, Aurélie? C'est toujours d'accord pour ce soir? On se retrouve au resto?**
a-loh o-ray-lee? say too-zhoor da-kor poor suh swar? oñ suh ruh-troov oh res-to?
Hello? Aurélie? Are you still OK for this evening? Shall we meet at the restaurant?

Aurélie **Désolée, mais je ne vais pas pouvoir venir. Je ne me sens pas très bien**
day-zo-lay, may zhuh nuh vay pa poov-war vuh-neer. zhuh nuh muh soñ pa tray byañ
I'm really sorry, but I'm not going to be able to come. I'm not feeling very well

Alain **Ah bon? Qu'est-ce qui ne va pas?**
a boñ? kess kee nuh va pa?
Oh yes? What's the problem?

Aurélie **J'ai mal à la tête et à la gorge, et je crois que j'ai un peu de fièvre**
zhay mal a la tet ay a la gorzh, ay zhuh krwa kuh zhay uñ puh duh fyeh-vruh
I've got a headache and sore throat and I think I have a slight temperature

Alain **Tu crois que tu as la grippe?**
too krwa kuh too a la greep?
Do you think you have flu?

Aurélie **Peut-être. Je vais aller à la pharmacie pour demander des conseils au pharmacien**
puht-et-ruh. zhuh vay a-lay a la far-ma-see poor duh-moñ-day day koñ-say oh far-mass-yañ
Maybe. I'm going to go to the chemist's to ask the pharmacist for some advice

Alain **Tu veux que je vienne avec toi?**
too vuh kuh zhuh vyen a-vek twa?
Do you want me to come with you?

Aurélie **Merci, c'est gentil, mais je vais y aller maintenant, et ensuite je vais aller me coucher**
mehr-see, say zhoñ-tee, may zhuh vay ee a-lay mañ-tuh-noñ, ay oñ-sweet zhuh vay a-lay muh koo-shay
Thanks, that's kind, but I'm going to go there now and then I'm going to go to bed

Alain **OK. Repose-toi bien. Je te rappellerai demain pour voir si ça va mieux**
o-kay. ruh-poz twa byañ. zhuh tuh ra-pel-uh-ray duh-mañ poor vwar see sa va myuh
OK. Have a good rest. I'll ring you again tomorrow to see if you're better

Aurélie **Merci. Et excuse-moi encore pour ce soir.**
On remettra ça à une prochaine fois
mehr-see. ay eks-kooz mwa oñ-kor poor suh swar.
oñ ruh-met-ra sa a oon pro-shen fwa
Thanks. And sorry again about tonight. We'll put it
off to the next time

Alain **Ne t'inquiète pas. Prends bien soin de toi!**
nuh tañk-yet pa. proñ byañ swañ duh twa!
Don't worry. Take good care of yourself!

OK, all right, agreed?

How do you ask if things are OK? Well, the word OK is often used
in informal French, along with the expressions we see here. One is
d'accord 'agreed, in agreement', as in c'est toujours d'accord?, 'is it
still OK?' (note that the word toujours, which you might think of as
'always', also means 'still'). The other involves the verb aller.
You'll probably be familiar with the informal expression ça va?
'OK?, are you OK?, is that OK?' The reply could be oui, ça va or non,
ça (ne) va pas! Here we have the question qu'est-ce qui ne va pas?
'what's wrong, what's the problem?'

Short talk

In conversational French people often shorten a word. Not only
by chopping off the end of it, as in prof for professeur, or sympa for
sympathique 'friendly, nice', but often by tacking on an -o to the
end: resto for restaurant, frigo for fridge (réfrigérateur), texto for
text message, even Macdo for Macdonalds.

from the dialogue

c'est toujours d'accord?
say too-zhoor da-kor?
is it still ok?

on se retrouve ...?
oñ suh ruh-troov
shall we meet ...?

au resto
oh rest-oh
at the restaurant

**je ne me sens pas très
bien**
zhuh nuh muh soñ pa tray byañ
I don't feel very well

j'ai mal à la tête
zhay mal a la tet
I've got a headache

un peu de fièvre
uñ puh duh fyev-ruh
a slight temperature

c'est gentil
say zhoñ-tee
that's kind

je vais y aller
zhuh vay ee a-lay
I'm going to go there

maintenant
mañ-tuh-noñ
now

je vais aller me coucher
zhuh vay a-lay muh koo-shay
I'm going to go to bed

repose-toi bien
ruh-poz twa byañ
have a good rest

une prochaine fois
oon pro-shen fwa
another time

ne t'inquiète pas
nuh tañk-yet pa
don't worry

How do you feel?

Je ne me sens pas très bien, says Aurélie – literally 'I don't feel myself very well'. When describing how you feel in French you need to use this 'reflexive' construction. If you remember from dialogue 12, the action in these is considered to be done to the same person who performs it, even when there doesn't seem to be any logical need for that. For example je m'intéresse aux voitures, 'I'm interested in cars' is literally 'I interest myself in cars'. A comparable English example might be 'I enjoyed myself'. Other examples with sentir might include je me sens un peu faible 'I feel a bit weak'; elle se sent en pleine forme 'she feels on top form'. > REFLEXIVE VERBS RefZone 32.

Proper poorly

In English we have a multitude of ways of saying we're unwell: you might have a headache, or a sore throat or a painful toe. The key term in French is mal 'pain', with the verb avoir 'to have' plus optionally the part of the body that's hurting. J'ai mal on its own means 'it hurts, I'm hurting'; to say where, you use à: j'ai mal à la tête 'I've got a headache', Aurélie a mal à la gorge 'Aurélie's got a sore throat', etc. Notice that if you want to specify two afflicted areas you need to repeat the à: j'ai mal à la tête et à la gorge, literally 'I have pain in the head and in the throat'. With the names of diseases, we sometimes use the definite article in English – 'do you think you've got (the) flu?' tu crois que tu as la grippe? – but you always need it in French.

Reflexives again

When giving direct orders to people, which needn't be rude in French, you use a command form of the verb called the imperative, which we see at the end of this dialogue in prends bien soin de toi!, 'take good care of youself'. But what if the verb in question is one of those that you 'do to yourself' rather than to someone else? When you want to make an order out of one of these ('enjoy yourself!') you tack the 'personal' bit onto the end of the verb, instead of before it. Let's take se reposer, 'to rest': je me repose 'I'm resting' tu te reposes 'you're resting', etc. The command would be repose-toi! 'Have a rest! Rest yourself!' – or using the more formal vous instead, reposez-vous! We've already heard it in the phrase installez-vous! 'sit down, settle yourselves in'.

Your place or mine?

How do you say you are going to a certain shop or office? Je vais aller à la pharmacie, says Aurélie. But she could have used a construction involving that little word chez, which refers not only to the place where someone lives, something like 'at/to the home of', but also anywhere they're based for work reasons. So aller chez le pharmacien would mean to go to the pharmacist's place, to go and see the chemist. J'ai oublié mon portefeuille chez le boulanger! 'I've left my wallet at the baker's!' Il faut que je passe chez le dentiste 'I must go and see the dentist, I must go by the dentist's place'.

Pharmacy first

Did you notice that Aurélie plans to go to the pharmacy to get some advice? In France this would probably be the first port of call. Pharmacists are medically trained and often able to supply suitable medication. All over-the-counter medicines are sold in pharmacies in France, not in supermarkets.

I have stomachache
j'ai mal à l'estomac
zhay mal a less-to-ma

my back hurts
j'ai mal au dos
zhay mal oh doh

she has earache
elle a mal à l'oreille
el a mal a lo-re-ee

he has toothache
il a mal aux dents
eel a mal oh doñ

I feel sick
j'ai envie de vomir
zhay oñ-vee duh vo-meer

I feel dizzy
j'ai des vertiges
zhay day ver-teezh

I'm pregnant
je suis enceinte
zhuh sweez oñ-sañt

he has high blood pressure
il fait de l'hypertension
eel fay duh lee-phr-toñss-yoñ

she's diabetic
elle est diabétique
el ay dya-bay-teek

I'm gluten intolerant
je ne supporte pas le gluten
zhuh nuh soo-port pa luh gloo-ten

I've cut my finger
je me suis coupé le doigt
zhuh muh swee koo-pay luh dwa

she bumped her head
elle s'est cogné la tête
el say kon-yay la tet

she had a fall
elle est tombée
el ay toñ-bay

now practise

(31)

> aches and pains

A visit to London

get to know ...

> informal French
> perfect and imperfect
> faire faire quelque chose
> geographical names

Bruno **Salut Pascal, comment ça va? Ça fait un certain temps que je t'ai pas vu**
sa-loo pas-kal, ko-moñ sa va? sa fay uñ sehr-tañ toñ kuh zhuh tay pa voo
Hi Pascal, how are you? I haven't seen you for a while

Pascal **Oui, j'étais à Londres pendant quelques jours**
wee, zhay-tay a loñ-druh poñ-doñ kel-kuh zhoor
Yes, I was in London for a few days

Bruno **Ça a été?**
sa a ay-tay?
How was it?

Pascal **Oui, c'était génial. Je me suis super bien amusé**
wee, say-tay zhen-yal. zhuh muh swee soo-pehr byañn am-oo-zay
It was great. I had a really brilliant time

Bruno **C'est pas cher, Londres?**
say pa shehr, loñ-druh?
Is London expensive?

Pascal **Si, mais j'ai logé chez des copains anglais très sympa qui m'ont fait
visiter Londres**
*see, may zhay lo-zhay shay day koh-pañ oñ-glay tray sañ-pa kee moñ fay
vee-zee-tay loñ-druh*
Yes it is, but I stayed with some really nice English pals who showed me
around London

Bruno **Et la bouffe, c'est dégueulasse, non?**
ay la boof, say day-guh-lass, non?
And what about the food, isn't it disgusting?

Pascal **Mais non, il y a de tout, on a mangé des repas italiens, chinois, indiens ...**
may noñ, eel ee a duh too, oñn a moñ-zhay day ruh-pa ee-tal-yañ, sheen-wa, añd-yañ ...
Not at all, you can get everything, we ate Italian, Chinese, Indian ...

Bruno **Justement, parce que la bouffe anglaise c'est dégueulasse!**
zhoos-tuh-moñ, parss-kuh la boof oñ-glez say day-guh-lass!
Exactly, because English food is disgusting!

Slangtastic!

The style of the language is different in this dialogue: Bruno and Pascal speak an informal style of French with various colloquial expressions. Such terms are widely heard in speech, not just among younger people, so it is as well to recognise them at least. There aren't always informal equivalents in English. Salut! ('hi!'), sympa ('nice, friendly'), dégueulasse ('disgusting') and la bouffe ('food') are common examples; you can find some more in the extra vocab section.

Getting tense

We've seen one kind of past tense, the one which covers things that have been done and accomplished and are now over. For example, Pascal has been to London and come back. The action of going to London is complete, and so he says je suis allé à Londres. In English you would say 'I went to London', rather than 'I was going', because at the time of speaking the business of going there is a clearly defined action that's now over and done with. But where the action is a comparatively long, gradual process that was in progress at the time being referred to, even if it has now finished, you use a tense called the imperfect: j'étais à Londres.

---

from the dialogue

comment ça va?
ko-moñ sa va?
how's it going?

pendant quelques jours
poñ-doñ kel-kuh zhoor
for a few days

ça a été?
sa a ay-tay?
was it good?

bien s'amuser
byañ sa-moo-zay
to have a good time

loger chez des copains
lo-zhay shay day koh-pañ
to stay with pals

il y a de tout
eel ee a duh too
there is everything

sympa
sañ-pa
nice

visiter
vee-zee-tay
to visit

la bouffe
la boof
food

dégueulasse
day-guh-las
disgusting

justement
zhoost-uh-moñ
exactly

How did it go?

One more informal expression it's good to know is the one Bruno uses to ask about whether the London trip had been a success: ça a été? – did it go OK? how was it?

Being a lodger

Languages have their little quirks, which can catch you out if you're not careful. You may know the verb rester meaning 'to stay' (not 'to rest'!), but this is stay in the sense of remain, not move or change. To stay meaning to spend the night somewhere, as in staying with friends, is loger.

Just visiting

How can you visit London if you're actually living there? Well, visiter is one of those slightly treacherous words that means something slightly different to the English word it resembles, in this case 'to visit'. It means to go to see a place or an attraction as a tourist, to 'go on a visit to' the place. To visit a person, for example going to their house on a social call, is rendre visite à.

Faire do's

Faire can be used in a similar way to English 'have', when you're talking about getting someone else to do something. If you have the car repaired or have your hair cut, it means you get someone to do it for you. In French to have something done is faire faire quelque chose, the first faire being equivalent to the English 'have'. For example, 'I'm going to have the car (la voiture) repaired' is je vais faire réparer la voiture. You can also use this expression to refer to friendly situations where no orders are given, but where someone invites you to do something: ils nous ont fait visiter Londres ('they had us visit London', ie they showed us round London).

extra vocabulary

great
formidable
for-mee-dabl

cool
génial
zhayn-yal

rubbish, useless
nul
nool

a bloke
un mec
uñ mek

the cops
les flics
lay fleek

work
le boulot
luh boo-loh

to eat
bouffer
boo-fay

car
la bagnole
la ban-yol

clothes
les fringues
lay frañg

Impersonal but informal

In informal French like this the impersonal word on is even more common than usual. It's often translated as 'one' or 'you', meaning anyone, the average person, but in spoken French it often just means 'we': on a mangé ... is just the same as nous avons mangé ... 'we ate ...'.

Changing names

Don't forget there are often French names for cities as well as countries, from Londres (London) to Édimbourg (Edinburgh) to Barcelone (Barcelona), to Venise (Venice/Venezia) – even some quite small places, like Douvres (Dover). Watch out for different spellings too, like Lyons (Lyon) which has no s in French. This can get quite confusing in Belgium, where the cities have French, Dutch and English names that are sometimes very different.

now practise

33

> **past tenses**

Word Zone (English–French)

A

a(n) un (m)/une (f)
able: to be able to pouvoir
about (approximately) vers ; environ
  (concerning) au sujet de
above au-dessus (de)
abroad à l'étranger
to accept accepter
accident l'accident (m)
address l'adresse (f)
adult l'adulte (m/f)
aeroplane l'avion (m)
afraid: to be afraid of avoir peur de
after après
afternoon l'après-midi (m)
again encore
age l'âge (m)
ago: a week ago il y a une semaine
AIDS le SIDA
airport l'aéroport (m)
all tout(e)/tous/toutes
allergic allergique
to allow permettre
  it's not allowed c'est interdit
all right (agreed) d'accord
  are you all right? ça va?
almost presque
alone tout(e) seul(e)
already déjà
also aussi
always toujours
a.m. du matin
America l'Amérique (f)
American américain(e)
and et
angry fâché(e)
anniversary l'anniversaire (m)
to announce annoncer
announcement l'annonce (f)
annual annuel(-elle)
another un(e) autre
answer la réponse
to answer répondre à
apartment l'appartement (m)
appendicitis l'appendicite (f)
apple la pomme

appointment le rendez-vous
approximately environ
apricot l'abricot (m)
April avril
are: you are vous êtes
  we are nous sommes
  they are ils/elles sont
arm le bras
to arrange arranger
arrival l'arrivée (f)
to arrive arriver
art gallery le musée
arthritis l'arthrite (f)
artist l'artiste (m/f)
to ask demander
  to ask a question poser une
  question
asparagus l'asperge (f)
aspirin l'aspirine (f)
asthma l'asthme (m)
  I have asthma je suis asthmatique
at à
  at my/your home chez moi/vous
  at 8 o'clock à huit heures
  at once tout de suite
Atlantic Ocean l'Océan atlantique (m)
attachment (to e-mail) la pièce jointe
attic le grenier
August août
aunt la tante
Australia l'Australie (f)
Australian australien(ne)
autumn l'automne (m)
available disponible
average moyen(ne)
to avoid éviter
awful affreux(-euse)

B

baby le bébé
back (of body) le dos
bacon le bacon ; le lard
bad (food, weather) mauvais(e)
bag le sac (suitcase) la valise
baggage les bagages (mpl)
baker's la boulangerie
balcony le balcon

bald (person) chauve
  (tyre) lisse
ball (large: football, etc) le ballon
  (small: golf, tennis, etc) la balle
balloon le ballon
banana la banane
bank (money) la banque
  (river) la rive ; le bord
bank account le compte en banque
bar le bar
basement le sous-sol
basket le panier
bath le bain
bathroom la salle de bains
battery (for car) la batterie
  (for radio, camera) la pile
bay (along coast) la baie
B&B la chambre d'hôte
to be être
beach la plage
beard la barbe
beautiful beau (belle)
because parce que
to become devenir
bed le lit
bedroom la chambre à coucher
beer la bière
before avant
to begin commencer
behind derrière
Belgian belge
Belgium la Belgique
to believe croire
bell (church, school) la cloche
  (doorbell) la sonnette
to belong to appartenir à
below sous
beside (next to) à côté de
best le/la meilleur(e)
better meilleur(e)
  better than meilleur que
between entre
bicycle la bicyclette ; le vélo
big grand(e), gros(se)
bill (restaurant) l'addition (f)
  (hotel) la note
  (for work done) la facture

bird l'oiseau *(m)*
biro le stylo
birth la naissance
birth certificate l'acte de naissance
birthday l'anniversaire *(m)*
bit: *a bit (of)* un peu (de)
to bite *(animal)* mordre
    (insect) piquer
black noir(e)
to bleed saigner
blind *(person)* aveugle
blond *(person)* blond(e)
blood le sang
blouse le chemisier
blue bleu(e)
boat le bateau
    (rowing) la barque
body le corps
book le livre
to book *(reserve)* réserver
booking la réservation
boring ennuyeux(-euse)
born: *to be born* naître
to borrow emprunter
both les deux
bottle la bouteille
box la boîte
boy le garçon
boyfriend le copain
bread le pain
to break casser
breakfast le petit déjeuner
bridge le pont
to bring apporter
Britain la Grande-Bretagne
British britannique
broken cassé(e)
brother le frère
brother-in-law le beau-frère
brown marron
brush la brosse
to build construire
to burn brûler
bus le bus
    (coach) le car
bus station la gare routière
bus stop l'arrêt de bus *(m)*
bus ticket le ticket de bus
business les affaires *(fpl)*
busy occupé(e)
but mais

butcher's la boucherie
butter le beurre
to buy acheter
by *(via)* par
    (beside) à côté de
    by bus en bus
    by car en voiture
    by train en train

C

cabin *(on boat)* la cabine
café le café
    internet café le cybercafé
cake *(large)* le gâteau
    (small) la pâtisserie ; le petit gâteau
call *(telephone)* l'appel *(m)*
to call *(speak, phone)* appeler
camera l'appareil photo *(m)*
    digital camera appareil photo numérique
to camp camper
campsite le camping
can *(to be able to)* pouvoir
    (to know how to) savoir
can la boîte
can opener l'ouvre-boîtes *(m)*
Canada le Canada
Canadian canadien(ne)
to cancel annuler
cancellation l'annulation *(f)*
capital *(city)* la capitale
car la voiture
car hire la location de voitures
car park le parking
carafe le pichet
caravan la caravane
card la carte
    birthday card la carte d'anniversaire
    playing cards les cartes à jouer
careful: *to be careful* faire attention
    careful! attention!
carpet *(rug)* le tapis
carriage *(railway)* la voiture
carrot la carotte
to carry porter
carton *(cigarettes)* la cartouche
    (milk, juice) le brick
case *(suitcase)* la valise
to cash *(cheque)* encaisser
cash desk la caisse
castle le château
cat le chat
to catch *(bus, train)* prendre

cathedral la cathédrale
CD le CD
CD player le lecteur de CD
cellar la cave
centimetre le centimètre
centre le centre
certain *(sure)* certain(e)
chair la chaise
change *(coins)* la monnaie
to change changer
    to change money changer de l'argent
    to change clothes se changer
    to change train changer de train
Channel *(English)* la Manche
charge *(fee)* le prix
to charge faire payer
cheap bon marché
cheaper moins cher
to check vérifier
to check in enregistrer
cheers! santé!
cheese le fromage
chemist's la pharmacie
cheque le chèque
cherry la cerise
chicken le poulet
child l'enfant *(m)*
children les enfants
chips les frites *(fpl)*
chocolate le chocolat
chocolates les chocolats *(mpl)*
to choose choisir
Christian name le prénom
Christmas Noël *(m)*
    merry Christmas! joyeux Noël!
Christmas card la carte de Noël
Christmas Eve la veille de Noël
church l'église *(f)*
cigarette la cigarette
cigarette lighter le briquet
cinema le cinéma
city la ville
city centre le centre-ville
clean propre
to clean nettoyer
clear clair(e)
client le client/la cliente
to climb faire de la montagne
clock l'horloge *(f)*
close by proche
to close fermer

closed (*shop, etc*) fermé(e)
cloth (*rag*) le chiffon
  (*fabric*) le tissu
clothes les vêtements (*mpl*)
coach (*bus*) le car ; l'autocar (*m*)
coat le manteau
code le code
coffee le café
  white coffee le café crème
  cappuccino le cappuccino
cold froid
  I'm cold j'ai froid
  it's cold il fait froid
cold (*illness*) le rhume
to collect (*someone*) aller chercher
colour la couleur
comb le peigne
to come venir
  (*to arrive*) arriver
  to come back revenir
  to come in entrer
  come in! entrez!
company (*firm*) la compagnie ;
  la société
to complain faire une réclamation
complaint la plainte
to complete remplir
compulsory obligatoire
computer l'ordinateur (*m*)
computer game le jeu électronique
concert le concert
concert hall la salle de concert
concession la réduction
conference la conférence
to confirm confirmer
confirmation la confirmation
congratulations! félicitations!
to consult consulter
to continue continuer
to cook (*be cooking*) cuisiner
  to cook a meal préparer un repas
cooker la cuisinière
cool frais (fraîche)
copy (*duplicate*) la copie
to copy copier
corkscrew le tire-bouchon
corner le coin
corridor le couloir
cost le coût
to cost coûter
cough la toux
to cough tousser
country (*not town*) la campagne

(*nation*) le pays
countryside le paysage
couple (*two people*) le couple
  a couple of... deux ...
course (*syllabus*) le cours
  (*of meal*) le plat
cousin le/la cousin(e)
crash (*car*) l'accident (*m*) ; la
  collision
cream (*food, lotion*) la crème
credit card la carte bleue
crisps les chips (*fpl*)
to cross (*road, etc*) traverser
crossing (*by sea*) la traversée
crossroads le carrefour
crowd la foule
cruise la croisière
to cry (*weep*) pleurer
crystal le cristal
cup la tasse
cupboard le placard
currency la devise ; la monnaie
curtain le rideau
custom (*tradition*) la tradition
customer le/la client(e)
customs la douane
to cut couper
to cycle faire du vélo

D

daily (*each day*) tous les jours
to dance danser
danger le danger
dangerous dangereux(-euse)
dark l'obscurité (*f*)
  after dark à la nuit tombée
date la date
date of birth la date de naissance
daughter la fille
daughter-in-law la belle-fille
day le jour
dead mort(e)
deaf sourd(e)
dear cher (chère) (*m(f)*)
December décembre
deep profond(e)
to defrost décongeler
delay le retard
delicatessen le traiteur (*f*)
delicious délicieux(-euse)
demonstration la manifestation

dentist le/la dentiste
to depart partir
department le rayon
department store le grand magasin
departure le départ
deposit les arrhes (*fpl*)
to describe décrire
desk (*furniture*) le bureau
  (*information*) l'accueil (*m*)
dessert le dessert
detour la déviation
to develop (*photos*) faire développer
to dial (*a number*) composer
dialling code l'indicatif (*m*)
diarrhoea la diarrhée
diary l'agenda (*m*)
dictionary le dictionnaire
to die mourir
diesel le gazole
diet le régime
difficult difficile
digital camera l'appareil photo
  numérique (*m*)
to dilute diluer
dining room la salle à manger
dinner (*evening meal*) le dîner
  to have dinner dîner
directions les indications (*fpl*)
  to ask for directions demander le
  chemin
directory (*telephone*) l'annuaire (*m*)
dirty sale
disabled (*person*) handicapé(e)
to disagree ne pas être d'accord
to disappear disparaître
to discover découvrir
dish le plat
district (*of town*) le quartier
to disturb déranger
diversion la déviation
divorced divorcé(e)
to do faire
doctor le médecin
documents les papiers (*mpl*)
dog le chien
domestic flight le vol intérieur
door la porte
doorbell la sonnette
down: to go down descendre
to download télécharger
downstairs en bas

drawing le dessin
dress la robe
to dress s'habiller
drink la boisson
to drink boire
drinking water l'eau potable (f)
to drive conduire
driver (of car) le conducteur/
la conductrice
to drown se noyer
drug (medicine) le médicament
(narcotics) la drogue
drunk ivre ; soûl(e)
dry sec (sèche)
to dry sécher
during pendant
duvet la couette
dye la teinture

E

each chacun/chacune
ear l'oreille (f)
earlier plus tôt
early tôt
to earn gagner
earphones le casque
earrings les boucles d'oreille (fpl)
earth la terre
east l'est (m)
Easter Pâques
happy Easter! joyeuses Pâques!
easy facile
to eat manger
egg l'œuf (m)
either ... or soit ... soit
elbow le coude
electrician l'électricien (m)
elevator l'ascenseur (m)
e-mail le e-mail ; le courriel
e-mail address l'adresse
électronique (f)
emergency l'urgence (f)
emergency exit la sortie de secours
empty vide
end la fin
engaged (to marry) fiancé(e)
(phone, toilet, etc) occupé(e)
engine le moteur
England l'Angleterre (f)
English anglais(e)
(language) l'anglais (m)

Englishman/-woman l'Anglais(e)
(m/f)
to enjoy aimer
enough assez
enquiry desk les renseignements
(mpl)
to enter entrer
entrance l'entrée (f)
error l'erreur (f)
to escape s'échapper
essential indispensable
euro l'euro (m)
Europe l'Europe (f)
European européen(ne)
European Union l'Union
européenne (f)
evening le soir
evening meal le dîner
every chaque
everyone tout le monde
everything tout
everywhere partout
examination l'examen (m)
example: for example par exemple
excellent excellent(e)
except sauf
to exchange échanger
exchange rate le taux de change
exciting passionnant(e)
excursion l'excursion (f)
excuse: excuse me! excusez-moi!
(to get by) pardon!
exhibition l'exposition (f)
exit la sortie
expenses les frais (mpl)
expensive cher (chère)
to expire (ticket, etc) expirer
to explain expliquer
express (train) le rapide
extension (electrical) la rallonge
extra (additional) supplémentaire
(more) de plus
eye l'œil (m)
eyes les yeux

F

face le visage
to faint s'évanouir
fair (hair) blond(e)
(just) juste
fair (funfair) la fête foraine
fake faux (fausse)

fall (autumn) l'automne (m)
to fall tomber
he has fallen il est tombé
family la famille
famous célèbre
fan (handheld) l'éventail (m)
(electric) le ventilateur
(sports) le supporter
far loin
is it far? c'est loin?
fare (bus, metro, etc) le prix du billet
farm la ferme
farmer le fermier
fast rapide
too fast trop vite
to fasten (seatbelt) attacher
fat gros (grosse)
(noun) la graisse
father le père
father-in-law le beau-père
fault (defect) le défaut
favourite préféré(e)
fax le fax
to fax (document) faxer
(person) envoyer un fax à
February février
to feed nourrir
to feel sentir
I feel sick j'ai la nausée
I don't feel well je ne me sens
pas bien
feet les pieds (mpl)
female (person) féminin
festival le festival
to fetch aller chercher
fever la fièvre
few peu
a few quelques-un(e)s
fiancé(e) le fiancé/la fiancée
to fight se battre
to fill remplir
to fill up (with petrol) faire le plein
film le film (for camera) la pellicule
to find trouver
fine (penalty) la contravention
finger le doigt
to finish finir
fire le feu ; l'incendie (m)
fire brigade les pompiers (mpl)
fireworks les feux d'artifice (mpl)
firm la compagnie
first premier(-ière)
first aid les premiers secours (mpl)

first-class de première classe
first name le prénom
fish le poisson
to fish pêcher
fishmonger's le/la marchand(e)
  de poisson
fit (medical) l'attaque (f)
to fit: it doesn't fit me ça ne me va pas
to fix (repair) réparer
  can you fix it? vous pouvez
  le réparer?
fizzy gazeux(-euse)
flag le drapeau
flat l'appartement (m)
flat tyre le pneu dégonflé
flavour le goût
  (of ice cream) le parfum
flight le vol
flood l'inondation (f)
floor (of room) le sol
  (storey) l'étage (m)
flour la farine
flower la fleur
flu la grippe
fly la mouche
to fly (person) aller en avion
  (bird) voler
fog le brouillard
foil le papier alu(minium)
to fold plier
to follow suivre
foot le pied
football le football
for pour
forbidden interdit(e)
forehead le front
foreign étranger(-ère)
foreigner l'étranger(ère) (m/f)
forever toujours
to forget oublier
fork (for eating) la fourchette
  (in road) l'embranchement (m)
form (document) le formulaire
fortnight la quinzaine
forward en avant
France la France
  in/to France en France
free (not occupied) libre
  (costing nothing) gratuit(e)
French français(e)
  (language) le français
fresh frais (fraîche)

Friday vendredi
fridge le frigo
fried frit(e)
friend l'ami(e) (m/f)
from de
front le devant
  in front of... devant...
fruit le fruit
fruit juice le jus de fruit
to fry frire
full plein(e)
  (occupied) complet(ète)
fun: to have fun s'amuser
funny (amusing) amusant(e)
furniture les meubles (mpl)
future l'avenir (m)

G

game le jeu
garage (for petrol) la station-service
  (for parking, repair) le garage
garden le jardin
gas le gaz
gay (person) homo
gear la vitesse
generous généreux(-euse)
gents (toilet) les toilettes pour
  hommes (fpl)
genuine authentique
German allemand(e)
  (language) l'allemand (m)
Germany l'Allemagne (f)
to get (obtain) obtenir
  (to fetch) aller chercher
to get in (vehicle) monter
to get off (bus, etc) descendre
gift le cadeau
girl la fille
girlfriend la copine
to give donner
to give back rendre
glass le verre
glasses les lunettes (fpl)
to go aller
to go back retourner
to go in entrer
to go out (leave) sortir
God Dieu (m)
gold l'or
good bon (bonne)
goodbye au revoir

good day bonjour
good evening bonsoir
goodnight bonne nuit
grandchildren les petits-enfants (mpl)
granddaughter la petite-fille
grandfather le grand-père
grandmother la grand-mère
grandparents les grands-parents (mpl)
grandson le petit-fils
great (big) grand(e)
  (wonderful) formidable
Great Britain la Grande-Bretagne
green vert(e)
grey gris(e)
grocer's l'épicerie (f)
ground la terre ; le sol
ground floor le rez-de-chaussée
guest (house guest) l'invité(e)
  (in hotel) le/la client(e)
guesthouse la pension
guide (tourist guide) le/la guide
guidebook le guide
guided tour la visite guidée

H

hair les cheveux (mpl)
hairdryer le sèche-cheveux
half la moitié
  half an hour une demi-heure
half fare le demi-tarif
half-price à moitié prix
ham (cooked) le jambon
  (cured) le jambon cru
hammer le marteau
hand la main
handbag le sac à main
handicapped handicapé(e)
handkerchief le mouchoir
handsome beau (belle)
to hang up (telephone) raccrocher
to happen arriver ; se passer
happy heureux(-euse)
  happy birthday! bon anniversaire!
harbour le port
hard (not soft) dur(e)
  (not easy) difficile
hardware shop la quincaillerie
hat le chapeau
to have avoir
to have to devoir
head la tête

headache le mal de tête
headlights les phares *(mpl)*
headphones les écouteurs *(mpl)*
health la santé
healthy sain(e)
to hear entendre
heart le cœur
heart attack la crise cardiaque
heating le chauffage
to heat up faire chauffer
heavy lourd(e)
heel le talon
height la hauteur
hello bonjour!
    (on telephone) allô?
helmet le casque
help! au secours!
to help aider
her son/sa/ses
here ici
    here is... voici...
to hide *(something)* cacher
    (oneself) se cacher
high haut(e)
hill la colline
hill walking la randonnée
him il ; lui
hire la location
    car hire la location de voitures
to hire louer
his son/sa/ses
to hit frapper
HIV le VIH
hobby le passe-temps
to hold tenir *(contain)* contenir
hold-up *(in traffic)* l'embouteillage *(m)*
hole le trou
holiday les vacances *(fpl)*
home la maison
    at my/your/our home chez
    moi/vous/nous
homosexual homosexuel(le)
honeymoon la lune de miel
to hope espérer
horse le cheval
hospital l'hôpital *(m)*
hot chaud(e)
    I'm hot j'ai chaud
    it's hot (weather) il fait chaud
hotel l'hôtel *(m)*
hour l'heure *(f)*
    half an hour une demi-heure

house la maison
house wine le vin en pichet
how? *(in what way)* comment?
    how much/many? combien?
    how are you? comment allez-vous?
hungry: *to be hungry* avoir faim
    I'm hungry j'ai faim
to hunt chasser
hurry: *I'm in a hurry* je suis pressé
to hurt: *that hurts* ça fait mal
husband le mari

I

ice la glace
    (cube) le glaçon
ice cream la glace
identity card la carte d'identité
if si
ignition key la clé de contact
ill malade
illness la maladie
immediately immédiatement
important important(e)
impossible impossible
to improve améliorer
in dans ; en ; à
    in 2 hours' time dans deux heures
    in France en France
    in Canada au Canada
    in London à Londres
in front of devant
included compris(e)
to increase augmenter
indicator *(car)* le clignotant
indigestion l'indigestion *(f)*
indoors à l'intérieur
information les renseignements *(mpl)*
to injure blesser
inside à l'intérieur
instead of au lieu de
insurance l'assurance *(f)*
to intend to avoir l'intention de
interesting intéressant(e)
internet l'internet *(m)*
    internet café le cybercafé
interval *(theatre)* l'entracte *(m)*
interview l'entrevue *(f)*
    (TV, etc) l'interview *(f)*
into dans ; en
    into town en ville
to introduce présenter
invitation l'invitation *(f)*

to invite inviter
Ireland l'Irlande *(f)*
Irish irlandais(e)
iron *(for clothes)* le fer à repasser
    (metal) le fer
ironmonger's la quincaillerie
is est
island l'île *(f)*
it il ; elle
Italian italien(ne)
Italy l'Italie *(f)*
item l'article *(m)*

J

jacket la veste
    waterproof jacket l'anorak *(m)*
jam *(food)* la confiture
jammed *(stuck)* coincé(e)
January janvier
jeans le jean
job le travail ; l'emploi *(m)*
to join *(become member)* s'inscrire
to join in participer
to joke plaisanter
journalist le/la journaliste
journey le voyage
jug le pichet
juice le jus
    orange juice le jus d'orange
July juillet
to jump sauter
June juin
just: *just two* deux seulement
    I've just arrived je viens d'arriver

K

to keep *(retain)* garder
key la clé
to kick donner un coup de pied à
kilo(gram) le kilo
kilometre le kilomètre
kind *(person)* gentil(-ille)
kind *(sort)* la sorte
to kiss embrasser
kitchen la cuisine
knee le genou
knife le couteau
to knock *(on door)* frapper
to knock down *(in car)* renverser
to knock over faire tomber
to know *(be aware of)* savoir

(person, place) connaître
I don't know je ne sais pas
I don't know Paris je ne connais pas Paris
to know how to do sth savoir faire quelque chose

L

ladder l'échelle (f)
lady la dame
lake le lac
to land atterrir
land la terre
language la langue
laptop le portable
large grand(e)
last dernier(-ière)
  last night (evening) hier soir
  (night-time) la nuit dernière
  last week la semaine dernière
  last year l'année dernière
late tard
  the train is late le train a du retard
later plus tard
to laugh rire
launderette la laverie automatique
lavatory les toilettes (fpl)
to learn apprendre
leather le cuir
to leave (depart for) partir
  (depart from) quitter
  (to leave behind) laisser
  to leave for Paris partir pour Paris
  to leave London quitter Londres
left: on/to the left à gauche
left-luggage (office) la consigne
leg la jambe
lemon le citron
lemonade la limonade
to lend prêter
length la longueur
lens (of camera, etc) l'objectif (m)
  (contact lens) la lentille
less moins
  less than moins de
lesson la leçon
to let (allow) permettre
  (to hire out) louer
letter la lettre
letterbox la boîte aux lettres
library la bibliothèque

licence le permis
to lie down s'allonger

lift (elevator) l'ascenseur (m)
light (not heavy) léger(-ère)
light la lumière
like (preposition) comme
  like this comme ça
to like aimer
  I'd like... je voudrais...
  we'd like... nous voudrions...
lip la lèvre
lipstick le rouge à lèvres
list la liste
to listen to écouter
litre le litre
litter (rubbish) les ordures (fpl)
little petit(e)
  a little... un peu de...
to live (in a place) vivre ; habiter
  I live in London j'habite à Londres
  he lives in a flat il habite dans un appartement
living room le salon
loaf le pain
to lock fermer à clé
locker (for luggage) le casier
London Londres
  to/in London à Londres
long long(ue)
  for a long time longtemps
to look after garder
to look at regarder
to look for chercher
lorry le camion
to lose perdre
lost (object) perdu(e)
lot: a lot of beaucoup de
lottery le loto
loud fort(e)
lounge (in hotel, airport) le salon
love l'amour (m)
to love (person) aimer
  (food, activity, etc) adorer
lovely beau (belle)
low bas (basse)
luck la chance
luggage les bagages (mpl)
lump (swelling) la bosse
lunch le déjeuner
lung le poumon

M

mad fou (folle)
magazine la revue

magnifying glass la loupe
maiden name le nom de jeune fille
mail le courrier
  by mail par la poste
main principal(e)
main course (of meal) le plat principal
to make faire
male (person) masculin
man l'homme (m)
to manage (to be in charge of) gérer
manager le/la directeur(-trice)
many beaucoup de
map la carte
  road map la carte routière
  street map le plan de la ville
March mars
mark (stain) la tache
market le marché
market place le marché
married marié(e)
match (game) la partie
matches les allumettes (fpl)
to matter: it doesn't matter ça ne fait rien
  what's the matter? qu'est-ce qu'il y a?
mattress le matelas
May mai
me moi
meal le repas
to mean vouloir dire
  what does this mean? qu'est-ce que ça veut dire?
meat la viande
medicine le médicament
to meet rencontrer
meeting la réunion
to melt fondre
member (of club, etc) le membre
membership card la carte de membre
memory la mémoire
  memory card la carte de mémoire
men les hommes (mpl)
to mend réparer
menu la carte
message le message
metre le mètre
metro le métro
midday midi
middle le milieu
midnight minuit
milk le lait

to mind: *do you mind if I...?* ça vous gêne si je...?
I don't mind ça m'est égal
do you mind? vous permettez?

mineral water l'eau minérale *(f)*

minute la minute

mirror le miroir
(in car) le rétroviseur

to miss *(train, flight, etc)* rater

Miss Mademoiselle

mistake l'erreur *(f)*

to mix mélanger

mobile phone le portable

Monday lundi

money l'argent *(m)*
I have no money je n'ai pas d'argent

money order le mandat

month le mois
this month ce mois-ci
last month le mois dernier
next month le mois prochain

moon la lune

more encore
more wine plus de vin

more than plus de
more than three plus de trois

morning le matin
in the morning le matin
this morning ce matin
tomorrow morning demain matin

mosquito le moustique

most (of the) la plupart (de)

mother la mère

mother-in-law la belle-mère

motor le moteur

motorbike la moto

motorway l'autoroute *(f)*

mountain la montagne

mountain bike le VTT

mouse *(animal, computer)* la souris

mouth la bouche

to move bouger

Mr Monsieur

Mrs Madame

Ms Madame

much beaucoup
too much trop

museum le musée

music la musique

musical *(show)* la comédie musicale

must devoir

my mon/ma/mes
my passport mon passeport
my room ma chambre
my suitcases mes valises

N

nail *(metal)* le clou
(finger) l'ongle *(m)*

name le nom
my name is... je m'appelle...

nappy la couche

narrow étroit(e)

nationality la nationalité

natural naturel(le)

nature reserve la réserve naturelle

navy blue bleu marine

near près de
is it near? c'est près d'ici?

necessary nécessaire

neck le cou

to need (to) avoir besoin de

needle l'aiguille *(f)*

neighbour le/la voisin(e)

nephew le neveu

net le filet
the net le net ; l'internet *(m)*

never jamais

new nouveau(-elle)

news *(TV, radio)* les informations *(fpl)*

newsagent's le magasin de journaux

newspaper le journal

New Year le Nouvel An
happy New Year! bonne année!

New Year's Eve la Saint-Sylvestre

New Zealand la Nouvelle-Zélande

next prochain(e)
(after) ensuite
the next train le prochain train
next week la semaine prochaine
next Monday lundi prochain
next to à côté de
we're going to Paris next ensuite nous allons à Paris

nice beau (belle)
(enjoyable) bon (bonne)
(person) sympathique

niece la nièce

night *(night-time)* la nuit
(evening) le soir
at night la nuit/le soir
last night hier soir
tomorrow night (evening) demain soir
tonight ce soir

nightclub la boîte de nuit

nightdress la chemise de nuit

no non
(without) sans
no thanks non merci
no ice sans glaçons
no sugar sans sucre

nobody personne

noise le bruit

none aucun(e)

non-smoking *(seat, compartment)* non-fumeurs

north le nord

Northern Ireland l'Irlande du Nord

nose le nez

not ne ... pas
I am not... je ne suis pas...

nothing rien
nothing else rien d'autre

notice *(warning)* l'avis *(m)*
(sign) le panneau

November novembre

now maintenant

nowhere nulle part

number *(quantity)* le nombre
(of room, house) le numéro

nurse l'infirmier/l'infirmière *(m/f)*

nut *(to eat)* la noix

O

to obtain obtenir

occupation *(work)* l'emploi *(m)*

ocean l'océan *(m)*

October octobre

odd *(strange)* bizarre

of de
a glass of... un verre de...
made of... en...

off *(light)* éteint(e)
(rotten) mauvais(e) ; pourri(e)

office le bureau

often souvent

oil *(for car, food)* l'huile *(f)*

OK! *(agreed)* d'accord!

old vieux (vieille)
how old are you? quel âge avez-vous?
I'm... years old j'ai... ans

on *(light)* allumé(e)
(engine, etc) en marche
on the table sur la table
on time à l'heure

once une fois
at once tout de suite

only seulement

open ouvert(e)

to open ouvrir

opposite en face de

or ou

orange *(fruit)* l'orange *(f)*
(colour) orange

orange juice le jus d'orange
to order (in restaurant) commander
to organize organiser
other autre
   have you any others? vous en
   avez d'autres?
our (sing) notre
   (plural) nos
out (light) éteint(e)
   he's/she's out il/elle est sorti(e)
outdoor (pool, etc) en plein air
outside dehors
oven le four
over (on top of) au-dessus de
to overtake (car) doubler ; dépasser
to owe devoir
   you owe me... vous me devez...
to own posséder
owner le/la propriétaire

P

to pack (luggage) faire les bagages
packet le paquet
page la page
paid payé(e)
   I've paid j'ai payé
pain la douleur
painful douloureux(-euse)
painkiller l'analgésique (m)
to paint peindre
panties la culotte
pants (underwear) le slip
paper le papier
parents les parents (mpl)
park le parc
to park garer (la voiture)
partner (business) l'associé(e) (m/f)
   (boy/girlfriend)
   le compagnon/la compagne
party (group) le groupe
   (celebration) la fête ; la soirée
   (political) le parti
pass (bus, train) la carte
   (mountain) le col
passenger le passager/la passagère
passport le passeport
password le mot de passe
path le chemin
patient (in hospital) le/la patient(e)
to pay payer
payment le paiement
payphone le téléphone public

peach la pêche
pear la poire
pen le stylo
pencil le crayon
pensioner le/la retraité(e)
people les gens (mpl)
per par
   per day par jour
   per hour à l'heure
   per person par personne
   per week par semaine
   100 km per hour 100 km à l'heure
perfect parfait(e)
perfume le parfum
perhaps peut-être
permit le permis
person la personne
pet l'animal domestique (m)
petrol l'essence (f)
petrol station la station-service
pharmacy la pharmacie
phone le téléphone
to phone téléphoner
phonebook l'annuaire (m)
phonebox la cabine (téléphonique)
phone call l'appel (m)
photograph la photo
to pick (choose) choisir
   (pluck) cueillir
picnic le pique-nique
picture (painting) le tableau
   (photo) la photo
piece le morceau
pill la pilule
pillow l'oreiller (m)
pink rose
pint: a pint of... un demi-litre de...
pity: what a pity quel dommage
place l'endroit (m)
place of birth le lieu de naissance
plain (unflavoured) ordinaire ; nature
to plan prévoir
plan (map) le plan
plane (aircraft) l'avion (m)
plate l'assiette (f)
platform (railway) le quai
to play (games) jouer
pleasant agréable
please s'il vous plaît
pleased content(e)
   pleased to meet you! enchanté(e)!
plenty of beaucoup de

p.m. de l'après-midi
pocket la poche
poison le poison
police (force) la police
policeman le policier
pool (swimming) la piscine
poor pauvre
port (seaport) le port
   (wine) le porto
possible possible
post (letters) le courrier
   by post par courrier
postbox la boîte aux lettres
postcard la carte postale
post office la poste
to postpone remettre à plus tard
potato la pomme de terre
pound (money) la livre
to pour verser
powder la poudre
power cut la coupure de courant
to prefer préférer
to prepare préparer
present (gift) le cadeau
pretty joli(e)
price le prix
print (photo) la photo
private privé(e)
prize le prix
probably probablement
problem le problème
professor le professeur d'université
programme (TV, etc) l'émission (f)
prohibited interdit(e)
to promise promettre
to provide fournir
public public(-ique)
public holiday le jour férié
pudding le dessert
to pull tirer
pullover le pull
puncture la crevaison
purple violet(-ette)
purse le porte-monnaie
to push pousser
pushchair la poussette
to put (place) mettre
pyjamas le pyjama

Q

quality la qualité

quantity la quantité
to quarrel se disputer
queen la reine
question la question
to queue faire la queue
quick rapide
quickly vite
quiet (place) tranquille
quite (rather) assez
(completely) complètement

R

race (people) la race
(sport) la course
radio la radio
railway le chemin de fer
railway station la gare
rain la pluie
to rain: it's raining il pleut
raincoat l'imperméable (m)
rare (uncommon) rare
(steak) saignant(e)
raspberry la framboise
rate (price) le tarif
raw cru(e)
razor le rasoir
to read lire
ready prêt(e)
real vrai(e)
receipt le reçu
reception (desk) la réception
receptionist le/la réceptionniste
to recognize reconnaître
to recommend recommander
to recover (from illness) se remettre
red rouge
to reduce réduire
reduction la réduction
to refuse refuser
regarding concernant
region la région
registration form la fiche
relationship les rapports (mpl)
to remain rester
remember se rappeler
to remove enlever
rent le loyer
to rent louer
rental la location
to repair réparer
to repeat répéter

to reply répondre
to require avoir besoin de
reservation la réservation
to reserve réserver
rest (relaxation) le repos
(remainder) le reste
to rest se reposer
restaurant le restaurant
retired retraité(e)
to return (to a place) retourner
(to return something) rendre
return ticket le billet aller retour
reverse gear la marche arrière
rheumatism le rhumatisme
rice le riz
rich riche
to ride (horse) faire du cheval
right (correct) exact(e)
right la droite
on/to the right à droite
ring (on finger) la bague
to ring (bell) sonner
ripe mûr(e)
river la rivière
road la route
roast rôti(e)
roof le toit
room (in house) la pièce
(in hotel) la chambre
(space) la place
rose la rose
round rond(e)
roundabout (traffic) le rond-point
route la route ; l'itinéraire (m)
rubber (material) le caoutchouc
(eraser) la gomme
rubbish les ordures (fpl)
rucksack le sac à dos
to run courir

S

sad triste
safe (for valuables) le coffre-fort
safe sûr ; sans danger
salary le salaire
salt le sel
same même
sand le sable
sandals les sandales (fpl)
sandwich le sandwich
toasted sandwich
le croque-monsieur

Saturday samedi
sauce la sauce
saucepan la casserole
to save (life) sauver
(money) épargner ; économiser
to say dire
scarf (headscarf) le foulard
(woollen) l'écharpe (f)
school l'école (f)
primary school l'école primaire
secondary school (11-15) le collège
(15-18) le lycée
scissors les ciseaux (mpl)
Scotland l'Écosse (f)
Scottish écossais(e)
screen l'écran (m)
screwdriver le tournevis
sea la mer
seafood les fruits de mer (mpl)
seaside le bord de la mer
season (of year, holiday time) la saison
seat (chair) le siège
(in train) la place
(cinema, theatre) le fauteuil
seatbelt la ceinture de sécurité
second second(e)
second-hand d'occasion
secretary le/la secrétaire
to see voir
to sell vendre
to send envoyer
senior citizen le/la senior
separated séparé(e)
September septembre
serious grave
to serve servir
service station la station-service
set menu le menu à prix fixe
settee le canapé
several plusieurs
to shake (bottle, etc) agiter
to share partager
to shave se raser
sheet (for bed) le drap
shelf le rayon
shirt la chemise
shoe la chaussure
shoeshop le magasin de
chaussures
shop le magasin
to shop faire du shopping
shop assistant le vendeur/

la vendeuse

shopping centre le centre commercial

short court(e)

shortly bientôt

shoulder l'épaule (f)

to shout crier

show le spectacle

to show montrer

shower (wash) la douche

shut (closed) fermé(e)

to shut fermer

sick (ill) malade

side le côté

sign (notice) le panneau

to sign signer

signature la signature

silk la soie

silver l'argent (m)

similar (to) semblable (à)

since depuis

to sing chanter

single (unmarried) célibataire
(bed, room) pour une personne

single ticket l'aller simple (m)

sink (washbasin) l'évier (m)

sister la sœur

sister-in-law la belle-sœur

to sit s'asseoir

size (clothes) la taille
(shoe) la pointure

to ski faire du ski

skin la peau

skirt la jupe

sky le ciel

to sleep dormir

slice (bread, cake, etc) la tranche

slide (photograph) la diapositive

to slip glisser

slow lent(e)

to slow down ralentir

slowly lentement

small petit(e)
smaller than plus petit(e) que

smell l'odeur (f)

to smile sourire

to smoke fumer

smooth lisse

snack le casse-croûte

snack bar le snack-bar

to sneeze éternuer

snow la neige

to snow: it's snowing il neige

soap le savon

socks les chaussettes (fpl)

soft doux (douce)

some de (du/de la/des)

someone quelqu'un

something quelque chose

sometimes quelquefois

son le fils

son-in-law le gendre

soon bientôt
as soon as possible dès que possible

sore douloureux(-euse)

sore throat: to have a sore throat avoir mal à la gorge

sorry: I'm sorry! excusez-moi!

sort la sorte
what sort? de quelle sorte?

soup le potage ; la soupe

south le sud

Spain l'Espagne (f)

Spanish espagnol(e)

sparkling (wine) mousseux(-euse)
(water) gazeux(-euse)

to speak parler

special spécial(e)

to spell: how is it spelt? comment ça s'écrit?

to spend (money) dépenser
(time) passer

to spill renverser

spoon la cuillère

spring (season) le printemps
(metal) le ressort

square (in town) la place

to squeeze presser

stairs l'escalier (m)

stamp le timbre

to stand (get up) se lever
(be standing) être debout

star l'étoile (f) (celebrity) la vedette

to start commencer

starter (in meal) le hors d'œuvre
(in car) le démarreur

station la gare

stay le séjour
enjoy your stay! bon séjour!

to stay (remain) rester
(reside for while) loger

to steal voler

stepdaughter la belle-fille

stepfather le beau-père

stepmother la belle-mère

stepson le beau-fils

stereo la chaîne (stéréo)

still: still water l'eau plate (f)

still (yet) encore

to sting piquer

stolen volé(e)

stomach l'estomac (m)

stomach ache: to have a stomach ache avoir mal au ventre

to stop arrêter

store (shop) le magasin

storey l'étage (m)

storm l'orage (m)

story l'histoire (f)

straightaway tout de suite

straight on tout droit

straw (for drinking) la paille

strawberries les fraises (fpl)

street la rue

street map le plan des rues

strong fort(e)

student (male) l'étudiant
(female) l'étudiante

stupid stupide

subtitles les sous-titres (mpl)

subway le passage souterrain

suddenly soudain

sugar le sucre

suit (man's) le costume
(woman's) le tailleur

suitcase la valise

summer l'été (m)

sun le soleil

Sunday le dimanche

sunny: it's sunny il fait beau

sunset le coucher de soleil

sunstroke l'insolation (f)

supermarket le supermarché

supplement le supplément

to supply fournir

to surf faire du surf
to surf the net surfer sur Internet

surname le nom de famille

surprise la surprise

to survive survivre

to swallow avaler

to sweat transpirer

sweatshirt le sweat-shirt

sweet sucré(e)

sweets les bonbons *(mpl)*
to swim nager
swimming pool la piscine
swimsuit le maillot de bain
Swiss suisse
switch le bouton
to switch off éteindre
to switch on allumer
Switzerland la Suisse

T

table la table
tablet le comprimé
to take *(something)* prendre
to take away *(something)* emporter
to take off *(clothes)* enlever
    (plane) décoller
to talk (to) parler (à)
tall grand(e)
tank *(petrol)* le réservoir
    (fish) l'aquarium *(m)*
tap le robinet
to taste goûter
taxi le taxi
tea le thé
teapot la théière
to teach enseigner
teacher le professeur
team l'équipe *(f)*
teeth les dents *(fpl)*
telephone le téléphone
to telephone téléphoner
telephone box la cabine téléphonique
television la télévision
to tell dire
temperature la température
    to have a temperature avoir de la
    fièvre
temporary temporaire
tenant le/la locataire
tent la tente
terrace la terrasse
to test *(try out)* tester
to text envoyer un message SMS
text message le message SMS à
to thank remercier
thank you merci
that cela
    that one celui-là/celle-là
the le/la/l'/les
theatre le théâtre

theft le vol
their *(sing)* leur
    (plural) leurs
there is/are... il y a...
thermometer le thermomètre
these ces
    these ones ceux-ci/celles-ci
they ils/elles
thick *(not thin)* épais(se)
thin *(person)* mince
thing la chose
    my things mes affaires
to think penser
thirsty: *I'm thirsty* j'ai soif
this ceci
    this one celui-ci/celle-ci
those ces
    those ones ceux-là/celles-là
throat la gorge
through à travers
thumb le pouce
thunderstorm l'orage *(m)*
Thursday jeudi
ticket le billet ; le ticket
tie la cravate
tight *(fitting)* serré(e)
tights le collant
till *(until)* jusqu'à
    till 2 o'clock jusqu'à deux heures
time le temps *(of day)* l'heure *(f)*
    this time cette fois
timetable l'horaire *(m)*
tin *(can)* la boîte
tip *(to waiter, etc)* le pourboire
tired fatigué(e)
to à *(with name of country)* en/au
    to London à Londres
    to the airport à l'aéroport
    to France en France
    to Canada au Canada
tobacconist's le tabac
today aujourd'hui
toe le doigt de pied
together ensemble
toilet les toilettes *(fpl)*
tomato la tomate
tomorrow demain
    tomorrow morning demain matin
    tomorrow afternoon demain
    après-midi
    tomorrow evening demain soir
tongue la langue
tonight ce soir

too *(also)* aussi
    it's too big c'est trop grand
    it's too hot il fait trop chaud
    it's too noisy il y a trop de bruit
tooth la dent
toothbrush la brosse à dents
toothpaste le dentifrice
top: *the top floor* le dernier étage
torch la lampe de poche
total *(amount)* le total
tough *(meat)* dur(e)
tour l'excursion *(f)*
    guided tour la visite guidée
tour guide le/la guide
tourist le/la touriste
tourist (information) office
    le syndicat d'initiative
towel la serviette
tower la tour
town la ville
town centre le centre-ville
town plan le plan de la ville
toy le jouet
traditional traditionnel(-elle)
traffic la circulation
traffic jam l'embouteillage *(m)*
traffic lights les feux *(mpl)*
train le train
trainers les baskets *(fpl)*
to translate traduire
to travel voyager
travel agent's l'agence de voyages *(f)*
tree l'arbre *(m)*
trip l'excursion *(f)*
trolley le chariot
trousers le pantalon
truck le camion
true vrai(e)
to try essayer
to try on *(clothes, etc)* essayer
Tuesday mardi
tunnel le tunnel
to turn tourner
to turn off *(light, etc)* éteindre
    (engine) couper le moteur
to turn on *(light, etc)* allumer
    (engine) mettre en marche
twice deux fois
to type taper à la machine
tyre le pneu
tyre pressure la pression des pneus

U

ugly laid(e)
umbrella le parapluie
uncle l'oncle (m)
uncomfortable inconfortable
under sous
underground le métro
underpants (man's) le caleçon
to understand comprendre
underwear les sous-vêtements (mpl)
to undress se déshabiller
unemployed au chômage
United Kingdom le Royaume-Uni
United States les États-Unis (mpl)
university l'université (f)
to unlock ouvrir
unpleasant désagréable
to unplug débrancher
to unscrew dévisser
up: to get up (out of bed) se lever
upside down à l'envers
upstairs en haut
to use utiliser
useful utile
usually d'habitude

V

vacancy (in hotel) la chambre
vacant libre
vacation les vacances (fpl)
van la camionnette
vase le vase
VAT la TVA
vegan végétalien(ne)
vegetables les légumes (mpl)
vegetarian végétarien(ne)
vehicle le véhicule
very très
vet le/la vétérinaire
via par
to video (from TV) enregistrer
village le village
visa le visa
to visit visiter
visitor le/la visiteur(-euse)
to vomit vomir

W

to wait for attendre
waiter le/la serveur(-euse)
waitress la serveuse
to wake up se réveiller
Wales le pays de Galles
walk la promenade
   to go for a walk faire une
   promenade
to walk aller à pied ; marcher
wall le mur
wallet le portefeuille
to want vouloir
war la guerre
ward (hospital) la salle
warm chaud(e)
to wash laver
   to wash oneself se laver
wasp la guêpe
watch la montre
to watch (look at) regarder
water l'eau (f)
way (manner) la manière
   (route) le chemin
way in (entrance) l'entrée (f)
way out (exit) la sortie
we nous
weak faible
   (coffee, etc) léger(-ère)
to wear porter
weather le temps
weather forecast la météo
web (internet) le Web
website le site web
wedding le mariage
Wednesday mercredi
week la semaine
   next week la semaine prochaine
weekday le jour de semaine
weekend le week-end
to weigh peser
welcome! bienvenu(e)!
well (healthy) en bonne santé
   he's not well il ne va pas bien
Welsh gallois(e)
west l'ouest (m)
wet mouillé(e)
what que ; quel/quelle ; quoi
wheel la roue
wheelchair le fauteuil roulant
when quand
   (at what time?) à quelle heure?
where où
which quel/quelle
   which (one)? lequel/laquelle?
which (ones)? lesquels/lesquelles?
white blanc (blanche)
who qui
whole entier(-ière)
why pourquoi
wide large
wife la femme
to win gagner
wind le vent
window la fenêtre (shop) la vitrine
windy: it's windy il y a du vent
wine le vin
winter l'hiver (m)
wire le fil
with avec
without sans
woman la femme
wonderful merveilleux(-euse)
wood le bois
word le mot
work le travail
to work (person) travailler
   (machine, car) fonctionner ; marcher
   it doesn't work ça ne marche pas
world le monde
worse pire
worth: it's worth... ça vaut...
to wrap (up) emballer
to write écrire
wrong faux (fausse)

X

X-ray la radiographie

Y

year l'an (m) ; l'année (f)
yellow jaune
yes oui
yesterday hier
yet: not yet pas encore
young jeune
your (familiar sing) ton/ta
   (familiar plural) tes
   (polite singular) votre
   (polite plural) vos
youth hostel l'auberge de jeunesse (f)

Z

zip la fermeture éclair
zoo le zoo

Word Zone (French-English)

A

à to ; at
abîmer to damage
accepter to accept
accident *m* accident
accompagner to accompany
accord *m* agreement
accueillir to greet ; to welcome
acheter to buy
addition *f* bill
adresse *f* address
adulte *m/f* adult
aéroport *m* airport
affaires *fpl* business ; belongings
affreux(-euse) awful
âge *m* age
agence *f* agency ; branch
agenda *m* diary
agent de police *m* police officer
agiter to shake
agréable pleasant ; nice
aider to help
aimer to like ; to love *(person)*
alarme *f* alarm
alcool *m* alcohol ; fruit brandy
alimentation *f* food
Allemagne *f* Germany
allemand(e) German
aller to go
aller (simple) *m* single ticket
aller retour *m* return ticket
allô? hello? *(on telephone)*
allumer to turn on ; to light
allumette *f* match
améliorer to improve
amer(-ère) bitter
américain(e) American
Amérique *f* America
ami(e) *m/f* friend
   petit(e) ami(e) boyfriend/girlfriend
amour *m* love
amusant(e) funny *(amusing)*
an *m* year
ancien(ne) old ; former
Anglais *m* Englishman

anglais *m* English *(language)*
anglais(e) English
Angleterre *f* England
animal *m* animal
année *f* year ; vintage
   bonne année! happy New Year!
anniversaire *m* anniversary ;
   birthday
annonce *f* advertisement
annuaire *m* directory
annuler to cancel
antenne *f* aerial
août August
appareil-photo *m* camera
appartement *m* apartment
appel *m* phone call
appeler to call *(speak, phone)*
appendicite *f* appendicitis
apporter to bring
apprendre to learn
appuyer to press
après after
après-midi *m* afternoon
arbre *m* tree
argent *m* money ; silver
argot *m* slang
armoire *f* wardrobe
arranger to arrange
arrêt *m* stop
arrêter to stop
arrière *m* rear ; back
arriver to arrive ; to happen
arrobase @ ; at sign
arrondissement *m* district
article *m* item ; article
artiste *m/f* artist
ascenseur *m* lift
aspirateur *m* vacuum cleaner
asseoir to sit (someone) down
   s'asseoir to sit down
assez enough ; quite *(rather)*
assiette *f* plate
assuré(e) insured
assurer to assure ; to insure
asthme *m* asthma
attacher to fasten *(seatbelt)*

attendre to wait (for)
attention! look out!
   faire attention to be careful
au-dessus de above ; on top of
au lieu de instead of
au secours! help!
aucun(e) none ; no ; not any
augmenter to increase
aujourd'hui today
aussi also
aussitôt immediately
   aussitôt que possible as soon
   as possible
Australie *f* Australia
australien(ne) Australian
autobus *m* bus
autocar *m* coach
automne *m* autumn
autorisé(e) permitted ; authorized
autoroute *f* motorway
autre other
avaler to swallow
avance *f* advance
   à l'avance in advance
avant before ; front
   à l'avant at the front
   en avant forward
avec with
avenir *m* future
avertir to inform ; to warn
avion *m* aeroplane
avis *m* notice ; warning
aviser to advise
avoir to have
avril April

B

bague *f* ring *(on finger)*
baignoire *f* bath *(tub)*
bain *m* bath
baisser to lower
balance *f* weighing scales
balle *f* ball *(small: golf, tennis)*
ballon *m* balloon ; ball *(large)* ; glass
banc *m* seat ; bench
banlieue *f* suburbs
banque *f* bank

barbe *f* beard

barrière *f* barrier

bas *m* bottom *(of page, etc)* ; stocking
  en bas below ; downstairs

bas(se) low

baskets *fpl* trainers

bassin *m* pond ; washing-up bowl

bateau *m* boat ; ship

bâtiment *m* building

batterie *f* battery *(for car)*

beau (belle) lovely ; handsome ;
  beautiful ; nice *(enjoyable)*

beaucoup (de) much/many ; a lot of

bébé *m* baby

belge Belgian

Belgique *f* Belgium

besoin: *avoir besoin de* to need

beurre *m* butter

bibliothèque *f* library

bien well ; right ; good

bientôt soon ; shortly

bienvenu(e) welcome!

bière *f* beer

bijouterie *f* jeweller's ; jewellery

billet *m* note ; ticket

biscuit *m* biscuit

blanc (blanche) white ; blank

blesser to injure

bleu *m* bruise

bleu(e) blue ; very rare *(steak)*
  bleu marine navy blue

blond(e) fair *(hair)*

bœuf *m* beef

boire to drink

bois *m* wood

boisson *f* drink

boîte *f* can ; box ; tin
  boîte à lettres post box
  boîte de conserve tin *(of food)*
  boîte de nuit night club

bon (bonne) good ; right ; nice
  bon anniversaire happy birthday
  bon marché inexpensive

bonbon *m* sweet

bonsoir good evening

bord *m* border ; edge ; verge
  à bord on board
  au bord de la mer at the seaside

bouche *f* mouth

bouché(e) blocked

boucherie *f* butcher's shop

bouchon *m* cork ; plug *(for sink)*

bouillir to boil

boulangerie *f* bakery

boule *f* ball

boules *fpl* game similar to bowls

bout *m* end

bouteille *f* bottle

bouton *m* button ; switch ; spot

bras *m* arm

Bretagne *f* Brittany

breton(ne) from Brittany

bricolage *m* do-it-yourself

briquet *m* cigarette lighter

britannique British

bronzage *m* suntan

brosse *f* brush
  brosse à cheveux hairbrush
  brosse à dents toothbrush

brouillard *m* fog

bru *f* daughter-in-law

bruit *m* noise

brûler to burn

brûlures d'estomac *fpl* heartburn

brun(e) brown ; dark

bureau *m* desk ; office

bus *m* bus

C

cabinet *m* office

cacher to hide

cadeau *m* gift

café *m* coffee ; café
  café au lait white coffee
  café crème white coffee
  café décaféiné decaff coffee

caisse *f* cash desk ; case

caissier(-ière) *m/f* cashier ; teller

calendrier *m* calendar ; timetable

camion *m* lorry ; truck

camionnette *f* van

campagne *f* countryside ; campaign

camper to camp

camping *m* camping ; camp-site

Canada *m* Canada

canadien(ne) Canadian

car *m* coach

carnet *m* notebook ; book
  carnet de billets book of tickets

carré *m* square

carrefour *m* crossroads

carte *f* map ; card ; menu ;
  pass *(bus, train)*
  carte bleue credit card

carte d'identité identity card
carte de crédit credit card
carte postale postcard

cartes (à jouer) *fpl* playing cards

casque *m* helmet

cassé(e) broken

casser to break

cassette *f* cassette

cathédrale *f* cathedral

cause *f* cause

caution *f* security *(for loan)* ; deposit

cave *f* cellar

CD *m* CD

ceci this

ceinture *f* belt
  ceinture de sécurité seatbelt

cela that

célèbre famous

célibataire single *(unmarried)*

cent *m* hundred

centime *m* cent

central(e) central

centre *m* centre
  centre commercial shopping centre
  centre-ville city centre

cercle *m* circle ; ring

certain(e) certain *(sure)*

cesser to stop

cette this ; that

ceux-ci/celles-ci these ones

ceux-là/celles-là those ones

chacun/chacune each

chaîne *f* chain ; channel

chaise *f* chair
  chaise de bébé high chair

chambre *f* bedroom ; room
  chambre d'hôte bed and breakfast

champ *m* field
  champ de courses racecourse

chance *f* luck

changement *m* change

changer to change
  se changer to change clothes

chanson *f* song

chanter to sing

chapeau *m* hat

chaque each ; every

charcuterie *f* pork butcher's ;
  delicatessen ; cooked meat

chasser to hunt

chat *m* cat

chaud(e) hot

chauffage *m* heating
chauffer to heat up *(milk, water)*
chauffeur *m* driver
chaussette *f* sock
chaussure *f* shoe ; boot
chauve bald *(person)*
chef *m* chef ; chief ; head ; leader
chemin *m* path ; lane ; track ; way
   chemin de fer railway
cheminée *f* chimney ; fireplace
chemise *f* shirt
chemisier *m* blouse
chèque *m* cheque
cher (chère) dear ; expensive
chercher to look for
   aller chercher to fetch ; to collect
cheval *m* horse
cheveux *mpl* hair
chez at the house of
   chez moi at my house
chien *m* dog
chirurgien *m* surgeon
choisir to choose
choix *m* range ; choice ; selection
chômage: *au chômage* unemployed
chose *f* thing
cidre *m* cider
ciel *m* sky
cinéma *m* cinema
circuit *m* round trip ; circuit
circuler to operate *(train, bus, etc)*
ciseaux *mpl* scissors
cité *f* city ; housing estate
citron *m* lemon
   citron vert lime
clair(e) clear ; light
classe *f* class
clé *f* key ; spanner
clef *f* key
client(e) *m/f* client ; customer
climatisation *f* air-conditioning
climatisé(e) air-conditioned
clinique *f* clinic *(private)*
cloche *f* bell
clou *m* nail *(metal)*
cocher to tick *(on form)*
code *m* code
   code postal postcode
   code confidentiel pin number
cœur *m* heart
coin *m* corner
colis *m* parcel

colle *f* glue
collège *m* secondary school
coller to stick ; to glue
combien how much/many
commande *f* order *(in restaurant)*
commander to order
comme like
commencer to begin
commissariat (de police) *m* police
   station
compagnie *f* firm ; company
compagnon *m* boyfriend
compartiment *m* compartment
   (train)
complet(-ète) full (up)
complètement completely
comporter to consist of
   se comporter to behave
composer to dial *(a number)*
comprendre to understand
compris(e) included
compte *m* number ; account
compter to count *(add up)*
comptoir *m* counter *(in shop, bar, etc)*
concurrent(e) *m/f* competitor
conducteur(-trice) *m/f* driver
conduire to drive
confirmer to confirm
confiture *f* jam ; preserve
congelé(e) frozen
connaître to know
conseil *m* advice ; council
conseiller to advise
conserver to keep ; to retain
consigne *f* deposit ; left luggage
consommation *f* drink
construire to build
contenir to contain
content(e) pleased
contenu *m* contents
continuer to continue
contrat *m* contract
contre against ; versus
contrôle *m* check
contrôler to check
contrôleur(-euse) *m/f* ticket inspector
copie *f* copy *(duplicate)*
copier to copy
corps *m* body
correspondance *f* connection
côté *m* side

   à côté de beside ; next to
coudre to sew
couleur *f* colour
couloir *m* corridor ; aisle
coup *m* stroke ; shot ; blow
couper to cut
cour *f* court ; courtyard
courant(e) common ; current
courir to run
courrier *m* mail ; post
courriel *m* e-mail
cours *m* lesson ; course ; rate
course *f* race *(sport)* ; errand
   faire des courses to go shopping
court(e) short
cousin(e) *m/f* cousin
couteau *m* knife
coûter to cost
coûteux(-euse) expensive
couvert *m* cover charge ; place setting
couvert(e) covered
couverture *f* blanket ; cover
cravate *f* tie
crayon *m* pencil
crème *f* cream *(food, lotion)*
   crème à raser shaving cream
crevaison *f* puncture
crier to shout
crime *m* crime ; offence ; murder
crise *f* crisis ; attack *(medical)*
   crise cardiaque heart attack
croire to believe
cru(e) raw
cuiller, cuillère *f* spoon
cuir *m* leather
cuisiné(e) cooked
cuisine *f* cooking ; cuisine ; kitchen
   faire la cuisine to cook
cuisiner to cook
cuisinier *m* cook
cuisinière *f* cook ; cooker
cuit(e) cooked
culotte *f* knickers
curieux(-euse) strange
curseur *m* cursor *(computer)*
cuvée *f* vintage

D

dame *f* lady
danger *m* danger
dangereux(-euse) dangerous

dans into ; in ; on
danser to dance
date f date (day)
    date de naissance date of birth
de from ; of ; some
début m beginning
décembre December
découvrir to discover
décrire to describe
défaire to unfasten ; to unpack
défaut m fault ; defect
défense de... no.../... forbidden
dégâts mpl damage
dehors outside ; outdoors
déjeuner m lunch
délicieux(-euse) delicious
demain tomorrow
demander to ask (for)
demi(e) half
dent f tooth
dentier m dentures
dentifrice m toothpaste
dentiste m/f dentist
départ m departure
dépasser to exceed ; to overtake
depuis since
déranger to disturb
dernier(-ère) last ; latest
derrière at the back ; behind
dès from ; since
    dès votre arrivée as soon as you
    arrive
désagréable unpleasant
descendre to go down ; to get off
désirer to want
désolé(e) sorry
dessous (de) underneath
dessus (de) on top (of)
destination f destination
    à destination de bound for
deux two
    deux fois twice
    les deux both
deuxième second
devant in front (of)
développer to develop
devenir to become
devoir to have to; to owe
diabétique diabetic
dictionnaire m dictionary
différent(e) different
difficile difficult

dimanche m Sunday
dîner to have dinner
dîner m dinner
dire to say ; to tell
directeur m manager ; headmaster
direction f management ; direction
discussion f argument
disparaître to disappear
disparu(e) missing (disappeared)
disponible available
disque m record ; disk
divorcé(e) divorced
docteur m doctor
doigt m finger
donner to give ; to give away
dormir to sleep
dos m back (of body)
douane f customs
douche f shower
douloureux(-euse) painful
doux (douce) mild ; gentle ; sweet
douzaine f dozen
drapeau m flag
droit m right (entitlement)
droit(e) right (not left) ; straight
droite f right-hand side
    à droite on/to the right
dur(e) hard ; hard-boiled ; tough
durée f duration

E

eau f water
échanger to exchange
échapper to escape
écharpe f scarf (woollen)
école f school
écossais(e) Scottish
Écosse f Scotland
écouter to listen to
écran m screen
écrire to write
église f church
électricien m electrician
emballer to wrap (up)
embouteillage m traffic jam
émission f programme
emploi m use ; job
emporter to take away
    à emporter take-away
emprunter to borrow
en some ; any ; in ; to ; made of

    en face de opposite
    en panne out of order
    en retard late
enchanté(e)! pleased to meet you!
encore still ; yet ; again
endommager to damage
endroit m place
enfant m/f child
enlever to take away/off
ennuyeux boring
enseigner to teach
ensemble together
ensuite next ; after that
entendre to hear
entier(-ière) whole
entre between
entrée f entrance ; admission ; starter
entreprise f firm ; company
entrer to come in ; to go in
entretien m maintenance ; interview
enveloppe f envelope
environ around ; about
envoyer to send
épais(se) thick
épargner to save (money)
épicerie f grocer's shop
épileptique epileptic
équipe f team
équipement m equipment
erreur f mistake
escalier m stairs
Espagne f Spain
espagnol(e) Spanish
espèce f sort
espérer to hope
essai m trial ; test
essayer to try ; to try on
essence f petrol
estomac m stomach
et and
étage m storey
état m state
    États-Unis United States
été m summer
éteindre to turn off
éteint(e) out (light)
étiquette f label
étoile f star
étranger(-ère) m/f foreigner
    à l'étranger overseas ; abroad
être to be

étroit(e) narrow ; tight
étudiant(e) *m/f* student
étudier to study
euro *m* euro
Europe *f* Europe
européen(ne) European
événement *m* occasion ; event
éviter to avoid
exact(e) right *(correct)*
examen *m* examination
excellent(e) excellent
expirer to expire
expliquer to explain
exposition *f* exhibition
exprès on purpose ; deliberately
extérieur(e) outside
extra top-quality ; first-rate

F

fabriquer to manufacture
face: *en face (de)* opposite
fâché(e) angry
facile easy
façon *f* way ; manner
faible weak
faim *f* hunger
  avoir faim to be hungry
faire to make ; to do
famille *f* family
fatigué(e) tired
faute *f* mistake ; foul *(football)*
fauteuil *m* armchair ; seat
  fauteuil roulant wheelchair
faux (fausse) fake ; false ; wrong
faxer to fax
félicitations *fpl* congratulations
femme *f* woman ; wife
fenêtre *f* window
fer *m* iron *(material, golf club)*
  fer à repasser iron *(for clothes)*
férié(e): *jour férié* public holiday
ferme *f* farmhouse ; farm
fermé(e) closed
fermer to close/shut ; to turn off
fermeture *f* closing
  fermeture Éclair® zip
fête *f* holiday ; fête ; party
feu *m* fire ; traffic lights
février February
fiancé(e) engaged *(to marry)*
ficelle *f* string

fièvre *f* fever
  avoir de la fièvre to have
  a temperature
fil *m* thread ; lead *(electrical)*
filet *m* net ; fillet *(of meat, fish)*
fille *f* daughter ; girl
film *m* film
fils *m* son
fin *f* end
fin(e) thin *(material)* ; fine *(delicate)*
fini(e) finished
finir to end ; to finish
flacon *m* bottle *(small)*
flamand(e) Flemish
fleur *f* flower
fleuriste *m/f* florist
fleuve *m* river
foie *m* liver
foire *f* fair
fois *f* time
  cette fois this time
folle mad
foncé(e) dark *(colour)*
fonctionner to work *(machine)*
fond *m* back *(of hall, room)* ; bottom
fondre to melt
force *f* strength
formidable great *(wonderful)*
fort(e) loud; strong
fou (folle) mad
foule *f* crowd
four *m* oven
fournir to supply
fraîche fresh ; cool ; wet *(paint)*
frais fresh ; cool
frais *mpl* costs ; expenses
français(e) French
Français(e) Frenchman/woman
frapper to hit ; to knock *(on door)*
frein *m* brake
freiner to brake
frère *m* brother
frigo *m* fridge
frit(e) fried
frites *fpl* French fries ; chips
froid(e) cold
fromage *m* cheese
frontière *f* border ; boundary
fruit *m* fruit
fumer to smoke

G

gagner to earn ; to win
galerie *f* art gallery ; arcade
gallois(e) Welsh
gant *m* glove
garage *m* garage
garçon *m* boy ; waiter
garder to keep ; to look after
gare *f* railway station
  gare routière bus terminal
garer to park
gâteau *m* cake ; gateau
gauche left
  à gauche to/on the left
gâteau *m* cake
gaz *m* gas
gazeux(-euse) fizzy
gelé(e) frozen
gendarme *m* policeman *(in rural areas)*
gendarmerie *f* police station
gendre *m* son-in-law
généreux(-euse) generous
genou *m* knee
gentil(-ille) kind *(person)*
gérant(e) *m/f* manager/manageress
glace *f* ice ; ice cream ; mirror
glacé(e) chilled ; iced
glaçon *m* ice cube
glisser to slip
gomme *f* rubber *(eraser)*
gorge *f* throat ; gorge
gosse *m/f* kid *(child)*
goût *m* flavour ; taste
goûter to taste
gramme *m* gram
grand(e) great ; high ; big ; tall
grand-mère *f* grandmother
grand-père *m* grandfather
Grande-Bretagne *f* Great Britain
grands-parents *mpl* grandparents
gras(se) fat ; greasy
gratuit(e) free of charge
grave serious
graver to burn *(CD)*
gravure *f* print *(picture)*
grillé(e) grilled
Grèce *f* Greece
grippe *f* flu
gris(e) grey
gros(se) big ; large ; fat

grotte f cave
groupe m group ; party ; band
guerre f war
guichet m ticket office ; counter
guide m guide ; guidebook

H

habiller to dress
  s'habiller to get dressed
habitant(e) m/f inhabitant
habiter to live (in)
habituel(le) usual ; regular
handicapé(e) disabled (person)
haut(e) high ; tall
heure f hour ; time of day
  à l'heure on time
heureux(-euse) happy
hier yesterday
historique historic
hiver m winter
hollandais(e) Dutch
homme m man
homo m gay (person)
hôpital m hospital
horaire m timetable ; schedule
horloge f clock
hors: hors de out of
  hors service out of order
hôte m host ; guest
hôtel m hotel
  hôtel de ville town hall
huile f oil
hypermarché m hypermarket

I

ici here
il y a... there is/are...
  il y a un défaut there's a fault
  il y a une semaine a week ago
île f island
immédiatement immediately
immeuble m building (offices, flats)
imprimer to print
incendie m fire
inclus(e) included ; inclusive
indicateur m guide ; timetable
infectieux(-euse) infectious
inférieur(e) inferior ; lower
infirmier(-ière) m/f nurse
informations fpl news ; information
ingénieur m/f engineer

inquiet(-iète) worried
installations fpl facilities
interdit forbidden
intéressant(e) interesting
intérieur: à l'intérieur indoors
introduire to insert
inutile useless ; unnecessary
invité(e) m/f guest
inviter to invite
irlandais(e) Irish
Irlande f Ireland
Irlande du Nord f Northern Ireland
Italie f Italy
italien(ne) Italian

J

jaloux(-ouse) jealous
jamais never
jambe f leg
jambon m ham
janvier January
Japon m Japan
jardin m garden
jaune yellow
jetable disposable
jeter to throw
jeu m game ; set (of tools, etc)
jeudi m Thursday
jeune young
joindre to join ; to enclose
joli(e) pretty
joue f cheek
jouer to play (games)
jouet m toy
jour m day
  jour férié public holiday
journal m newspaper
journée f day (length of time)
juillet July
juin June
jupe f skirt
jusqu'à (au) until ; till
juste fair ; reasonable

K

kilo m kilo
kilomètre m kilometre

L

là there

lac m lake
laid(e) ugly
laine f wool
laisser to leave
lait m milk
lame f blade
lampe f light ; lamp
langue f tongue ; language
large wide ; broad
largeur f width
lavabo m washbasin
  lavabos toilets
lave-linge m washing machine
laver to wash
  se laver to wash oneself
laverie automatique f launderette
lave-vaisselle m dishwasher
leçon f lesson
léger(-ère) light ; weak (tea, etc)
légume m vegetable
lendemain m next day
lent(e) slow
lentement slowly
lettre f letter
  lettre recommandée registered letter
leur(s) their
lever to lift
  se lever to get up (out of bed)
lever de soleil m sunrise
lèvre f lip
librairie f bookshop
libre free ; vacant
libre-service self-service
lieu m place (location)
ligne f line ; service ; route
lire to read
liste f list
lit m bed
litre m litre
livraison f delivery (of goods)
livre f pound
livre m book
loger to stay (reside for while)
loin far
lointain(e) distant
loisir m leisure
Londres London
long(ue) long
longtemps for a long time
longueur f length
lot m prize ; lot (at auction)

louer to let ; to hire ; to rent
  à louer for hire/to rent
lourd(e) heavy
lumière *f* light
lundi *m* Monday
lune *f* moon
lunettes *fpl* glasses
lycée *m* secondary school

M

Madame *f* Mrs ; Ms ; Madam
Mademoiselle *f* Miss
magasin *m* shop
  grand magasin department store
mai May
maigre lean *(meat)*
maigrir to slim
maillot *m* vest
  maillot de bain swimsuit
main *f* hand
maintenant now
maire *m* mayor
mairie *f* town hall
mais but
maison *f* house ; home
mal badly
mal *m* harm ; pain
  mal de mer seasickness
  mal de tête headache
malade sick *(ill)*
maladie *f* disease
maman *f* mummy
manger to eat
manque *m* shortage ; lack
manteau *m* coat
maquillage *m* make-up
marche *f* step ; march; walking
marché *m* market
marcher to walk ; to work
mardi *m* Tuesday
  mardi gras Shrove Tuesday
mari *m* husband
mariage *m* wedding
marié *m* bridegroom
marié(e) married
mariée *f* bride
marier to marry
  se marier to get married
marquer to score *(goal, point)*
marron brown
mars March
masculin male *(person, on forms)*

match de football *m* football match
matériel *m* equipment ; kit
matin *m* morning
mauvais(e) bad ; wrong ; off *(food)*
méchant(e) naughty ; wicked
médecin *m* doctor
médicament *m* medicine ; drug
meilleur(e) best ; better
  meilleurs vœux best wishes
mél *m* e-mail address
membre *m* member *(of club, etc)*
même same
menu *m* menu *(set price)*
mer *f* sea
  mer du Nord North Sea
merci thank you
mercredi *m* Wednesday
mère *f* mother
merveilleux(-euse) wonderful
messieurs *mpl* men
mesurer to measure
météo *f* weather forecast
mètre *m* metre
métro *m* underground
mettre to put ; to put on
meubles *mpl* furniture
midi *m* midday ; noon
mieux better ; best
milieu *m* middle
mille *m* thousand
millimètre *m* millimetre
million *m* million
mince slim ; thin
minuit *m* midnight
minute *f* minute
miroir *m* mirror
mobilier *m* furniture
mode *f* fashion
  mode d'emploi instructions for use
moi me
moins less ; minus
mois *m* month
moitié *f* half
molle soft
moment *m* moment
mon/ma/mes my
monde *m* world
monnaie *f* currency ; change
monsieur *m* gentleman
Monsieur *m* Mr ; sir
montagne *f* mountain

montre *f* watch
montrer to show
morceau *m* piece ; bit
mordu(e) bitten
mort(e) dead
mot *m* word ; note *(letter)*
  mot de passe password
moteur *m* engine ; motor
  moteur de recherche search engine
motif *m* pattern
moto *f* motorbike
mou (molle) soft
mouche *f* fly
mouchoir *m* handkerchief
mouillé(e) wet
mourir to die
mousseux(-euse) sparkling *(wine)*
moustique *m* mosquito
moyen(ne) average
moyenne *f* average
mur *m* wall
mûr(e) mature ; ripe
musée *m* museum
  musée d'art art gallery
musique *f* music

N

nager to swim
naissance *f* birth
natation *f* swimming
nationalité *f* nationality
nature *f* wildlife
naturel(le) natural
né(e) born
neige *f* snow
neiger to snow
nettoyer to clean
neuf (neuve) new
neveu *m* nephew
nez *m* nose
nièce *f* niece
niveau *m* level ; standard
noce *f* wedding
nocturne *m* late opening
Noël *m* Christmas
  joyeux Noël! merry Christmas!
noir(e) black
nom *m* name ; noun
nombre *m* number
nombreux(-euse) numerous
non no ; not

nord *m* north

normal(e) normal ; standard *(size)*

notaire *m* solicitor

note *f* note ; bill ; memo

nourrir to feed

nourriture *f* food

nouveau (nouvelle) new
   de nouveau again

nouvelles *fpl* news

novembre November

nu(e) naked ; bare

nuit *f* night

numéro *m* number ; act ; issue

O

objet *m* object

obligatoire compulsory

obtenir to get ; to obtain

occasion *f* occasion ; bargain

occupé(e) busy ; hired *(taxi)* ;
  engaged *(toilet)*

octobre October

œuf *m* egg

office *m* service *(church)* ; office

offre *f* offer

œil *m* eye

ombre *f* shade/shadow
  à l'ombre in the shade

oncle *m* uncle

ongle *m* nail *(finger)*

opéra *m* opera

or *m* gold

orage *m* storm

orange orange ; amber *(traffic light)*

orange *f* orange

ordinaire ordinary

ordinateur *m* computer

ordonnance *f* prescription

ordre *m* order
  à l'ordre de payable to

ordures *fpl* litter *(rubbish)*

oreille *f* ear

oreiller *m* pillow

organiser to organize

os *m* bone

ou or

où where

oublier to forget

ouest *m* west

oui yes

outils *mpl* tools

ouvert(e) open ; on *(tap, gas, etc)*

ouverture *f* overture ; opening

ouvre-boîtes *m* tin-opener

ouvre-bouteilles *m* bottle-opener

ouvrir to open

P

page *f* page

pain *m* bread ; loaf of bread

pair(e) even

paire *f* pair

paix *f* peace

panier *m* basket

panne *f* breakdown

panneau *m* sign

pantalon *m* trousers

pantoufles *fpl* slippers

papier *m* paper
  papier hygiénique toilet paper

Pâques *m or fpl* Easter

paquet *m* package ; packet

par by ; through ; per
  par example for example

parapluie *m* umbrella

parc *m* park

parce que because

parcours *m* route

pare-brise *m* windscreen

parent(e) *m/f* relative

parents *mpl* parents

paresseux(-euse) lazy

parfait(e) perfect

parfum *m* perfume ; flavour

parking *m* car park

parler (à) to speak (to) ; to talk (to)

partager to share

parterre *m* flowerbed

parti *m* political party

partie *f* part ; match *(game)*

partir to leave ; to go
  à partir de from

partout everywhere

pas not
  pas encore not yet

pas *m* step ; pace

passager(-ère) *m/f* passenger

passé(e) past

passe-temps *m* hobby

passeport *m* passport

passer to pass ; to spend *(time)*
  se passer to happen

passionnant(e) exciting

patient(e) *m/f* patient *(in hospital)*

pâtisserie *f* cake shop ; little cake

patron(ne) *m/f* boss

pauvre poor

payer to pay (for)

pays *m* land ; country
  du pays local

Pays-Bas *mpl* Netherlands

paysage *m* countryside ; scenery

péage *m* toll *(motorway, etc)*

pêche *f* peach ; fishing

pêcher to fish

peigne *m* comb

peignoir *m* dressing gown

peindre to paint ; to decorate

peinture *f* painting ; paintwork

pellicule *f* film *(for camera)*

pencher to lean

pendant during

pendant que while

péninsule *f* peninsula

penser to think

pension *f* guesthouse
  pension complète full board

perdre to lose

perdu(e) lost *(object)*

père *m* father

permettre to permit

permis *m* permit ; licence

personne *f* person

peser to weigh

pétillant(e) fizzy

petit(e) small ; slight
  petit déjeuner breakfast

petit-fils *m* grandson

petite-fille *f* granddaughter

pétrole *m* oil *(petroleum)* ; paraffin

peu little ; few
  à peu près approximately
  un peu (de) a bit (of)

peur *f* fear
  avoir peur (de) to be afraid (of)

peut-être perhaps

pharmacie *f* chemist's ; pharmacy

photo *f* photograph

photocopier to photocopy

pichet *m* jug ; carafe

pièce *f* room ; play ; coin
  pièce d'identité means of
  identification
  pièce jointe attachment *(e-mail)*

pied *m* foot
  à pied on foot
pierre *f* stone
piéton *m* pedestrian
pile *f* pile ; battery
piquer to sting
piqûre *f* insect bite ; injection ; sting
pire worse
piscine *f* swimming pool
placard *m* cupboard
place *f* square *(in town)* ; seat
plage *f* beach
plaisir *m* enjoyment ; pleasure
plan *m* map *(of town)*
  plan de la ville street map
planche *f* plank
plante *f* plant ; sole
plaque *f* sheet ; plate
  plaque d'immatriculation
  numberplate
plat *m* dish ; course *(of meal)*
  plat de résistance main course
  plat principal main course
plat(e) level *(surface)* ; flat
  à plat flat *(battery)*
plateau *m* tray
plein(e) (de) full (of)
pleurer to cry *(weep)*
pleuvoir to rain
plier to fold
plomb *m* lead ; fuse
plombage *m* filling *(in tooth)*
plombier *m* plumber
plonger to dive
pluie *f* rain
plus more ; most
  plus grand(e) (que) bigger (than)
  plus tard later
plusieurs several
pneu *m* tyre
poche *f* pocket
poème *m* poem
poids *m* weight
poignet *m* wrist
point *m* place ; point ; stitch ; dot
pointure *f* size *(of shoes)*
poisson *m* fish
poissonnerie *f* fishmonger's shop
poitrine *f* breast ; chest
poivre *m* pepper
police *f* policy *(insurance)* ; police
policier *m* policeman ; detective

film/novel
pomme *f* apple
pomme de terre *f* potato
pompier *m* fireman
  pompiers fire brigade
pont *m* bridge ; deck *(of ship)*
  faire le pont to have a long
  weekend
populaire popular
port *m* harbour ; port
portable *m* mobile phone ; laptop
porte *f* door ; gate
portefeuille *m* wallet
porter to wear; to carry
porte-bagages *m* luggage rack
porte-monnaie *m* purse
poser to put ; to lay down
posséder to own
poste *f* post ; post office
poster to post
pot *m* pot ; carton
potable ok to drink
potage *m* soup
poubelle *f* dustbin
poudre *f* powder
poule *f* hen
poulet *m* chicken
poumon *m* lung
pour for
pourboire *m* tip
pourquoi why
pourri(e) rotten *(fruit, etc)*
pousser to push
poussette *f* push chair
pouvoir to be able to
préfecture de police *f* police
  headquarters
préféré(e) favourite
préférer to prefer
premier(-ière) first
prendre to take ; to get ; to catch
prénom *m* first name
préparer to prepare ; to cook
près de near (to)
présenter to present ; to introduce
pression *f* pressure
prêt(e) ready
prêter to lend
prière de... please...
principal(e) main
printemps *m* spring

priorité *f* right of way
prise *f* plug ; socket
privé(e) private
prix *m* price ; prize
  prix de détail retail price
probablement probably
problème *m* problem
prochain(e) next
proche close *(near)*
produits *mpl* produce ; product
professeur *m* teacher
profiter de to take advantage of
profond(e) deep
promenade *f* walk ; ride *(in vehicle)*
promettre to promise
propre clean ; own
propriétaire *m/f* owner
provisions *fpl* groceries
provisoire temporary
provisoirement for the time being
proximité: *à proximité* nearby
public(-ique) public
publicité *f* advert *(on TV)*
pull *m* sweater

Q

quai *m* platform
qualité *f* quality
quand when
quantité *f* quantity
quart *m* quarter
quartier *m* neighbourhood ; district
que that ; than ; whom ; what
quel(le) which ; what
quelqu'un someone
quelque some
quelque chose something
quelquefois sometimes
qui who ; which
quinzaine *f* fortnight
quoi what

R

radio *f* radio
radiographie *f* X-ray
rafraîchissements *mpl*
  refreshments
raide steep
raisin *m* grapes
  raisins secs sultanas ; raisins ;
  currants

raison *f* reason

ralentir to slow down

rappel *m* reminder *(on signs)*

rappeler to remind
  se rappeler to remember

rapide quick ; fast

rapide *m* express train

raser to shave off
  se raser to shave

rasoir *m* razor

rater to miss *(train, flight etc)*

rayé(e) striped

rayon *m* shelf ; department *(in store)*

RC ground floor

récemment recently

réception *f* reception ; check-in

réceptionniste *m/f* receptionist

recette *f* recipe

recharger to recharge *(battery, etc)*

réclame *f* advertisement

recommander to recommend

récompense *f* reward

reconnaître to recognize

reçu *m* receipt

réduction *f* reduction ; discount

réduire to reduce

refuser to reject ; to refuse

regarder to look at

régime *m* diet *(slimming)*

règlement *m* regulation ; payment

régler to pay ; to settle

rembourser to refund

remercier to thank

remettre to put back
  se remettre to recover *(from illness)*

remplir to fill ; to fill in/out/up

rencontrer to meet

rendez-vous *m* date ; appointment

rendre to give back

renouveler to renew

renseignements *mpl* information

rentrée *f* return to work/school

renverser to knock down *(in car)*

réparations *fpl* repairs

réparer to fix *(repair)*

repas *m* meal

repasser to iron

répondre (à) to reply ; to answer

réponse *f* answer ; reply

repos *m* rest
  se reposer to rest

réservation *f* reservation ; booking

réservé(e) reserved

réserver to book *(reserve)*

réservoir *m* tank

respirer to breathe

restaurant *m* restaurant

reste *m* rest *(remainder)*

rester to remain ; to stay

retard *m* delay

retirer to withdraw ; to collect *(tickets)*

retour *m* return

retourner to go back

retrait *m* withdrawal ; collection

retraité(e) retired

réunion *f* meeting

réussir (à) to succeed

réveil *m* alarm clock

réveiller to wake *(someone)*
  se réveiller to wake up

réveillon *m* Christmas/
  New Year's Eve

revenir to come back

rez-de-chaussée *m* ground floor

rhume *m* cold *(illness)*

riche rich

rideau *m* curtain

rien nothing ; anything

rire to laugh

robe *f* gown ; dress

robinet *m* tap

roman *m* novel

rond(e) round

rose pink

rose *f* rose

rôti(e) roast

roue *f* wheel
  roue de secours spare wheel

rouge red

rouge à lèvres *m* lipstick

rouler to roll ; to go *(by car)*

route *f* road ; route
  route nationale trunk road
  route principale major road
  route secondaire minor road

Royaume-Uni *m* United Kingdom

rue *f* street

S

sable *m* sand

sac *m* sack ; bag
  sac à dos backpack
  sac à main handbag

sac de couchage sleeping bag

sage good *(well-behaved)* ; wise

saigner to bleed

saint(e) *m/f* saint

Saint-Sylvestre *f* New Year's Eve

saisir to seize

saison *f* season
  de saison in season
  haute saison high season

salaire *m* salary ; wage

sale dirty

salé(e) salty ; savoury

salle *f* lounge *(airport)* ; hall ; ward
  salle à manger dining room
  salle d'attente waiting room
  salle de bains bathroom

salon *m* sitting room ; lounge

samedi *m* Saturday

sandwich *m* sandwich

sang *m* blood

sans without

santé *f* health
  santé! cheers!
  en bonne santé well

sapeurs-pompiers *mpl* fire brigade

sauf except (for)

sauter to jump

sauver to rescue

savoir to know *(be aware of)*

savon *m* soap

séance *f* meeting ; performance

sec (sèche) dried *(fruit, beans)*

sèche-cheveux *m* hairdryer

sèche-linge *m* tumble dryer

sécher to dry

seconde *f* second *(in time)*

secouer to shake

secours *m* help

secrétaire *m/f* secretary

séjour *m* stay ; visit

sel *m* salt

semaine *f* week

sens *m* meaning ; direction

sentier *m* footpath

sentir to feel

septembre September

séparément separately

serrer to grip ; to squeeze
  serrez à droite keep to the right

serrure *f* lock

serveur *m* waiter

serveuse *f* waitress

service *m* service ; service charge
serviette *f* towel ; briefcase
servir to dish up ; to serve
seul(e) alone ; lonely
seulement only
si if ; yes *(to negative question)*
SIDA *m* AIDS
siècle *m* century
siège *m* seat ; head office
signaler to report
signer to sign
simple simple ; single ; plain
site *m* site
   site web web site
situé(e) located
ski *m* ski ; skiing
slip *m* underpants ; panties
société *f* company ; society
sœur *f* sister
soif *f* thirst
   avoir soif to be thirsty
soin *m* care
soir *m* evening
soirée *f* evening ; party
sol *m* ground ; soil
soleil *m* sun ; sunshine
somme *f* sum
sonnette *f* doorbell
sorte *f* kind *(sort, type)*
sortie *f* exit
   sortie de secours emergency exit
sortir to go out *(leave)*
soudain suddenly
souhaiter to wish
sourd(e) deaf
sourire to smile
souris *f* mouse
sous underneath ; under
sous-sol *m* basement
sous-titres *mpl* subtitles
souterrain(e) underground
soutien-gorge *m* bra
souvent often
spectacle *m* show *(in theatre)*
spectateurs *mpl* audience
sportif(-ive) sports ; athletic
stade *m* stadium
stage *m* course
station *f* station *(metro)* ; resort
   station de taxis taxi rank
   station-service service station

stationnement *m* parking
stylo *m* pen
sucre *m* sugar
sucré(e) sweet
sud *m* south
suisse Swiss
Suisse *f* Switzerland
suivant(e) following
suivre to follow
supermarché *m* supermarket
supplément *m* extra charge
supplémentaire extra
sur on ; onto ; on top of ; upon
   sur place on the spot
sûr safe ; sure
surcharger to overload
surchauffer to overheat
surf *m* surfing
   faire du surf to surf
surveillé(e) supervised
sympa(thique) nice ; pleasant
syndicat d'initiative *m* tourist office

T

tabac *m* tobacco ; tobacconist's
table *f* table
tableau *m* painting ; picture ; board
taille *f* size *(of clothes)* ; waist
tailleur *m* tailor ; suit
talon *m* heel ; stub *(counterfoil)*
tante *f* aunt
taper to strike ; to type
tapis *m* carpet
tard late
   au plus tard at the latest
tarif *m* price-list ; rate ; tarif
tasse *f* cup ; mug
taux *m* rate
TCF *m* Touring Club de France *(AA)*
teinturerie *f* dry cleaner's
télé *f* TV
télécharger to download
télécommande *f* remote control
téléphone *m* telephone
téléphoner (à) to phone
téléviseur *m* television (set)
télévision *f* television
température *f* temperature
tempête *f* storm
temps *m* weather ; time
tenir to hold ; to keep

tente *f* tent
terrain *m* ground ; land ; pitch ;
   course
terre *f* land ; earth ; ground
tête *f* head
TGV *m* high-speed train
thé *m* tea
ticket *m* ticket *(bus, cinema, museum)*
timbre *m* stamp
tire-bouchon *m* corkscrew
tirer to pull
tiroir *m* drawer
tissu *m* material ; fabric
toilettes *fpl* toilet ; powder room
toit *m* roof
tomber to fall
tordre to twist
tôt early
total *m* total *(amount)*
toucher to touch
toujours always ; still ; forever
tour *f* tower
tour *m* trip ; walk ; ride
tourisme *m* sightseeing
tourner to turn
tournevis *m* screwdriver
tous all *(plural)*
   tous les jours daily
tousser to cough
tout(e) all ; everything
   tout à l'heure in a while
   tout compris all inclusive
   tout de suite straight away
tout le monde everyone
toutes all *(plural)*
   toutes directions all routes
toux *f* cough
traditionnel(-elle) traditional
traduction *f* translation
traduire to translate
train *m* train
tranche *f* slice
tranquille quiet *(place)*
transpirer to sweat
travail *m* work
travailler to work *(person)*
travaux *mpl* road works ; alterations
travers: à travers through
traverser to cross *(road, sea)*
très very ; much
triste sad
trop too ; too much

trottoir *m* pavement ; sidewalk

trou *m* hole

trouver to find
  se trouver to be *(situated)*

tuer to kill

tuyau *m* pipe *(for water, gas)*

TVA *f* VAT

U

UE *f* EU

ultérieur(e) later *(date, etc)*

un(e) one ; a ; an

Union européenne *f* European Union

université *f* university

urgence *f* urgency ; emergency

usine *f* factory

utile useful

utiliser to use

V

vacances *fpl* holiday(s)
  en vacances on holiday

vaccin *m* vaccination

valable valid *(ticket, licence, etc)*

valeur *f* value

valise *f* suitcase

valoir to be worth
  ça vaut... it's worth...

vapeur *f* steam

vedette *f* speedboat ; star *(film)*

végétal(e) vegetable

végétarien(ne) vegetarian

véhicule *m* vehicle

vélo *m* bike

vendange(s) *fpl* harvest *(of grapes)*

vendeur(-euse) *m/f* sales assistant

vendre to sell
  à vendre for sale

vendredi *m* Friday

vénéneux poisonous

venir to come

vent *m* wind

vente *f* sale

ventilateur *m* ventilator ; fan

vérifier to check ; to audit

verre *m* glass

vers toward(s) ; about

versement *m* payment ; instalment

verser to pour ; to pay

vert(e) green

veste *f* jacket

vêtements *mpl* clothes

veuf *m* widower

veuillez... please...

veuve *f* widow

viande *f* meat

vide empty

vie *f* life

vieux (vieille) old

VIH *m* HIV

village *m* village

ville *f* town ; city

vin *m* wine

violet(-ette) purple

virage *m* bend ; curve ; corner

visage *m* face

visite *f* visit ; consultation *(of doctor)*

visiter to visit *(a place)*

visiteur(-euse) *m/f* visitor

vite quickly ; fast

vitesse *f* gear *(of car)* ; speed

vivre to live

voie *f* lane (of road) ; line ; track

voir to see

voisin(e) *m/f* neighbour

voiture *f* car ; coach (of train)

vol *m* flight ; theft

voler to fly *(bird)* ; to steal

voleur(-euse) *m/f* thief

vomir to vomit

vouloir to want

voyage *m* journey

voyager to travel

vrai(e) real ; true

vue *f* view ; sight

W

wagon *m* carriage ; waggon

wagon-couchettes *m* sleeping car

X

xérès *m* sherry

Y

yacht *m* yacht

yaourt *m* yoghurt

yeux *mpl* eyes

Z

zéro *m* zero

zoo *m* zoo

Reference Zone

This section gives you the nuts and bolts – everything from alphabet and numbers to telling the time, plus the grammar bits including nouns, adverbs, pronouns and verb tables. Each topic has its own track and is illustrated with examples.

Alphabet (a, b, c)

The French alphabet contains the same letters as the English one, though some letters are much less common than in English, such as **k** and **w**, and of course some can take accents (**é**, **à** and so on). The pronunciation of the names of the letters is shown below.

a	*a*	n	*en*
b	*bay*	o	*oh*
c	*say*	p	*pay*
d	*day*	q	*koo*
e	*uh*	r	*ehr*
f	*eff*	s	*ess*
g	*zhay*	t	*tay*
h	*ash*	u	*oo*
i	*ee*	v	*vay*
j	*zhee*	w	*doo-bluh-vay*
k	*ka*	x	*eeks*
l	*el*	y	*ee-grek*
m	*em*	z	*zed*

how do you spell it?	**comment ça s'écrit?**
	ko-moñ sa say-kree?
it's spelt ...	**ça s'écrit ...**
	sa say-kree ...
in capitals/in small letters	**en majuscules/en minuscules**
	oñ ma-zhoo-skool/oñ mee-noo-skool
full stop/comma	**point/virgule**
	pwañ/veer-gool
all one word	**en un seul mot**
	oñn uñ suhl mo

---

need to know

French makes less use of capital letters than English, so remember not to use them in days, months and languages.

Numbers (1, 2, 3)

In grammar terms, these are known as 'cardinals' and they operate the same way in French as in English. Some differences occur in how they are written.

> **need to know**
>
> Currency symbols such as pound and euro signs (£, €) tend to be given after the number, rather than before as in English.

In French prices and decimals are written with a comma instead of a dot or full stop as in English. And thousands in French are separated by a full stop rather than a comma. In long numbers such as phone numbers, it's common practice in French to separate them into groups of two digits for convenience.

a 1.6 litre engine **un moteur de 1,6 litres**

01.40.20.50.50 **zéro un quarante vingt cinquante cinquante**

€10,000.00 **10.000,00 €**

0	**zéro** *zay-roh*
1	**un** *uñ*
2	**deux** *duh*
3	**trois** *trwa*
4	**quatre** *kat-ruh*
5	**cinq** *sañk*
6	**six** *seess*
7	**sept** *set*
8	**huit** *weet*
9	**neuf** *nuhf*
10	**dix** *deess*
11	**onze** *oñz*
12	**douze** *dooz*
13	**treize** *trehz*
14	**quatorze** *ka-torz*
15	**quinze** *kañz*
16	**seize** *sez*
17	**dix-sept** *dees-set*
18	**dix-huit** *deez-weet*
19	**dix-neuf** *dees-nuhf*
20	**vingt** *vañ*
21	**vingt et un** *vañt-ay-uñ*
22	**vingt-deux** *vañ-duh*

30	trente	*troñt*
40	quarante	*ka-roñt*
50	cinquante	*sañ-koñt*
60	soixante	*swa-soñt*
70	soixante-dix	*swa-soñt-deess*
71	soixante et onze	*swa-soñt ay oñz*
72	soixante-douze	*swa-soñt-dooz*
80	quatre-vingts	*kat-ruh-vañ*
81	quatre-vingt-un	*kat-ruh-vañ-uñ*
90	quatre-vingt-dix	*kat-ruh-vañ-deess*
91	quatre-vingt-onze	*kat-ruh-vañ-oñz*
100	cent	*soñ*
110	cent dix	*soñ deess*
200	deux cents	*duh soñ*
250	deux cent cinquante	*duh soñ sañ-koñt*
500	cinq cents	*sañk-soñ*
1,000	mille	*meel*
2,000	deux mille	*duh meel*
1,000,000	un million	*uñ meel-yoñ*

---

need to know

In some French-speaking areas (such as Belgium and Switzerland) a few numbers have different names, such as septante for 70 and nonante for 90.

he lives at number 10	**il habite au dix** *eel a-beet oh deess*
on page 19	**à la page dix-neuf** *a la pazh deez-nuhf*
in chapter 7	**au chapitre sept** *oh sha-peet-ruh set*
the year 2006	**l'an deux mille six** *loñ duh meel seess*
I'm 20 (years old)	**j'ai vingt ans** *zhay vañt oñ*

---

need to know

With people's ages, you have to give the word ans – you can't just say il a huit for 'he's eight'.

Numbers (1st, 2nd, 3rd)

In grammar terms, these are known as 'ordinals' since they give the order that things come in. They are also adjectives, but unlike most adjectives in French they come before the noun.

Generally speaking they are made by adding -ième to the number (deux, trois, etc), along with a u if the number ends in -q (cinquième), and replacing a final f with a -v (neuf – neuvième). If the number ends in -e, the -e disappears (quatre – quatrième).

1st	**premier (1er), première (1ère)** *pruhm-yay, pruhm-yehr*	
2nd	**deuxième** *duhz-yem*	
3rd	**troisième** *trwaz-yem*	
4th	**quatrième** *katree-yem*	
5th	**cinquième** *sañk-yem*	
6th	**sixième** *seez-yem*	
7th	**septième** *set-yem*	
8th	**huitième** *weet-yem*	
9th	**neuvième** *nuhv-yem*	
10th	**dixième** *deez-yem*	
11th	**onzième** *oñz-yem*	
12th	**douzième** *dooz-yem*	
13th	**treizième** *trez-yem*	
14th	**quatorzième** *ka-torz-yem*	
15th	**quinzième** *kañz-yem*	
16th	**seizième** *sez-yem*	
17th	**dix-septième** *dee-set-yem*	
18th	**dix-huitième** *deez-weet-yem*	
19th	**dix-neuvième** *deez-nuhv-yem*	
20th	**vingtième** *vañt-yem*	
21st	**vingt et unième** *vañt-ay-uñn-yem*	
22nd	**vingt-deuxième** *vañt-duhz-yem*	
100th	**centième** *soñt-yem*	

on the first of December	**le premier décembre** *luh pruhm-yay day-soñb-ruh*
he came in third	**il est arrivé troisième** *eel ayt a-ree-vay trwaz-yem*
he lives on the fifth floor	**il habite au cinquième étage** *eel a-beet oh sañk-yem ay-tazh*

Time (telling the time)

When talking about clock time, the time of day, the word is **l'heure** (think of 'the hour' in old-fashioned English). The French often use the 24-hour clock.

To give the time, use the phrase **il est** for 'it is', followed by the number and **heure(s)** – so literally 'one hour', 'seven hours' etc:

 it's one o'clock **il est une heure**
 it's two o'clock **il est deux heures**

For times 'to' the hour you use **moins**:

 five to ten **dix heures moins cinq**
 at quarter to seven **à sept heures moins le quart**

For times 'past' the hour, you can just name the number of minutes past, though with quarter and half past, the word **et** 'and' is needed:

 ten past one **une heure dix**
 quarter past one **une heure et quart**
 half past one **une heure et demie**

---

need to know

In English you can leave out 'o'clock' – 'it's nearly eight' – but French always includes the word **heure(s)** – you can't just say **il est presque huit**.

---

what time is it?	**quelle heure est-il?**
	kel uhr ayt-eel
do you have the right time?	**vous avez l'heure exacte?**
	vooz a-vay luhr eg-zakt?
at what time?	**à quelle heure?**
	a kel uhr
at midnight	**à minuit**
	a meen-wee
at midday, at noon	**à midi**
	a mee-dee
at nine o'clock at night	**à neuf heures du soir**
	a nuhv uhr doo swar
at 11.15	**à 11h15, à onze heures quinze**
	a oñz uhr kañz
at 8.45pm	**à 20h45, à vingt heures quarante-cinq**
	a vañt uhr karoñt-sañk

Time (in general)

The word 'time' covers a lot of meanings in English: 'time is money', 'three times', 'what time is it?' These are all different senses of the word which have different translations in French.

Time in general is **le temps**, but a time in the sense of an occasion or repetition is **la fois**:
> I haven't got time **je n'ai pas le temps**
> the first/next/last time **la première/prochaine/dernière fois**

Both **en** and **dans** can be used in French to specify a length of time, but the meaning is very different:
> **je le ferai dans trois jours** I'll do it in three days (ie in three days' time, three days from now)
> **je le ferai en trois jours** I'll do it in three days (ie within three days)

'Ago' is rendered by the phrase **il y a**:
> **je l'ai fait il y a trois jours** I did it three days ago

'For' and 'since' are expressed using **depuis**:
> **j'apprends le français depuis deux mois** I've been learning French for two months
> **j'apprends le français depuis octobre** I've been learning French since October

---

need to know

Il y a **can also mean 'there is/are' – don't get confused!**

sometimes	**quelquefois** *kel-kuh-fwa*
all the time	**tout le temps** *too luh toñ*
from time to time	**de temps en temps** *duh toñz oñ toñ*
early	**tôt** *toh*
early (ie before time, too soon)	**en avance** *oñn a-voñss*
it's late (ie getting on)	**il est tard** *eel ay tar*
late (ie behind time)	**en retard** *oñ ruh-tar*
on time	**à l'heure** *a luhr*

Days of the week

Days of the week are masculine and are not written with a capital letter in French. The French for 'day' is **le jour**.

Monday	**lundi** *luñ-dee*	Friday	**vendredi** *voñ-druh-dee*
Tuesday	**mardi** *mar-dee*	Saturday	**samedi** *sam-dee*
Wednesday	**mercredi** *mehr-kruh-dee*	Sunday	**dimanche** *dee-moñsh*
Thursday	**jeudi** *zhuh-dee*		

> **need to know**
>
> **Le week-end** is one of the most established borrowings in French, as in **bon week-end!**

To say that something happens *on* Monday, you just use the name of the day on its own:
je l'ai vu lundi I saw him on Monday
mercredi je vais à Paris on Wednesday I'm going to Paris

If you add the definite article **le lundi** you mean *every* Monday, on Mondays:
je la vois le lundi I see her on Mondays

The article is also used when giving a range of days:
du lundi 17 au vendredi 28 janvier from Monday 17 to Friday 28 January

every Monday	**tous les lundis** *too lay luhñ-dee*
last Tuesday	**mardi dernier** *mar-dee dehrn-yay*
next Friday	**vendredi prochain** *voñ-druh-dee pro-shañ*
a week on Saturday	**samedi en huit** *sam-dee oñ weet*
today/tomorrow/yesterday	**aujourd'hui/demain/hier** *oh-zhoor-dwee/duh-mañ/ee-yehr*

Months and seasons

Months and seasons are masculine in French, and are not written with a capital letter. The French for 'month' is **le mois**.

January	**janvier** *zhoñ-vyay*	July	**juillet** *zhwee-yay*
February	**février** *fayv-ree-ay*	August	**août** *oot*
March	**mars** *marss*	September	**septembre** *sep-toñb-ruh*
April	**avril** *av-reel*	October	**octobre** *ok-tob-ruh*
May	**mai** *may*	November	**novembre** *noh-voñb-ruh*
June	**juin** *zhwañ*	December	**décembre** *day-soñb-ruh*

spring	**le printemps** *luh prañ-toñ*	autumn	**l'automne** *loh-ton*
summer	**l'été** *lay-tay*	winter	**l'hiver** *lee-vehr*

in February	**en février** *oñ fayv-ree-ay*
next September	**en septembre prochain** *oñ sep-toñb-ruh pro-shañ*
on 1 December	**le premier (1er) décembre** *luh pruhm-yay day-soñ-bruh*
in 2006	**en deux mille six** *oñ duh meel seess*
Monday 26 February	**lundi vingt-six (26) février** *luhñ-dee vañt-seess fayv-ree-ay*
my birthday is on 16 September	**mon anniversaire est le seize (16) septembre** *moñn a-nee-vehr-sehr ay luh sayz sep-toñ-bruh*
in spring/in winter	**au printemps/en hiver** *oh prañ-toñ/oñn ee-vehr*

Quantities (a kilo, a tin)

Quantities in French are followed by **de** 'of', never ~~**du, de la** or **des**~~.

a litre of wine	**un litre de vin** *uñ lee-truh duh vañ*
half a litre of milk	**un demi-litre de lait** *uñ duh-mee lee-truh duh lay*
200 grams of ham	**deux cents grammes de jambon** *duh soñ gram duh zhoñ-boñ*
half a kilo of cherries	**un demi-kilo de cerises** *uñ duh-mee kee-loh duh suh-reez*
a kilo of oranges	**un kilo d'oranges** *uñ kee-loh do-roñzh*
a bottle of water	**une bouteille d'eau** *oon boo-tay doh*
a glass of cognac	**un verre de cognac** *uñ vehr duh kon-yak*
a tin of tomatoes	**une boîte de tomates** *oon bwat duh to-mat*
a carton of orange juice	**une brique de jus d'orange** *oon breek duh joo do-roñzh*
a jar of honey	**un pot de miel** *uñ poh duh myel*
a slice of cake	**une tranche de gâteau** *oon troñsh duh ga-toh*
more ...	**plus de ...** *ploos duh ...*
less ...	**moins de ...** *mwañ duh ...*
enough ...	**assez de ...** *assay duh ...*

need to know

The word **livre** 'pound' *(feminine)* can apply to the metric pound of 500g as well as the imperial one, not to mention the pound sterling.

Nouns and articles (a dog)

Nouns are labels for anything you can give a name to: 'market', 'cheese', 'house'. It doesn't have to be a solid thing. It can be something abstract like 'morning', or it can be the name of something specific like a person or place: 'Mary', 'Manchester' (such nouns, spelt with a capital letter, are called 'proper' nouns). In French nouns have a gender – they can be either masculine or feminine.

French nouns are either masculine (**le**) or feminine (**la**). Therefore words for 'the' (**le** and **la**) and 'a', 'an' (**un** and **une**) must agree with the noun they accompany – whether masculine, feminine or plural. In grammar terms they are known as 'articles'.

	masculine	feminine	plural
the	**le chat**	**la rue**	**les chats, les rues**
a, an	**un chat**	**une rue**	**des chats, des rues**

If the noun begins with a vowel (a, e, i, o or u) or an unsounded h, **le** and **la** shorten to **l'**, ie **l'avion** (m), **l'école** (f), **l'hôtel** (m).

Although French nouns are masculine or feminine, this doesn't mean that the thing itself necessarily has male or female characteristics. For example 'person' is **la personne** and 'victim' is **la victime**. To find out the gender of a word you will need to look it up, but sometimes you can make an educated guess from its ending.

When there is more than one of something, the 'plural' form is used; in English, this most often involves adding an -s (markets, mornings, cheeses) though many words have irregular plurals (man/men, sheep/sheep). Adding an -s is also the standard way to make a plural in French, though there are quite a few exceptions, such as nouns ending in -**eau**, -**eu** and -**al**, which take -**x** in the plural: **le bateau-les bateaux, le neveu-les neveux, le cheval-les chevaux**. Nouns ending in -**s**, -**x**, or -**z** don't change in the plural: **un bus-des bus** 'bus-buses'.

Typically masculine endings include:

-er, -ier, -ien, -eau, -t, -c, -ail, -oir, -é, -acle, -age, -ège, -ème, -o, -ou

winter **l'hiver**
paper **le papier**
dog **le chien**
boat **le bateau**
packet **le paquet**
block **le bloc**
detail **le détail**

manor le manoir
café le café
miracle le miracle
storm l'orage
college le collège
problem le problème
kilo le kilo
nail le clou

Typically feminine endings include:

-euse, -trice, -ière, -ienne, -elle, -te, -tte, -de, -che, -aille, -oire, -ée, -té, -tié, -onne, -aison, -ion, -esse, -ie, -ine, -une, -ure, -ance, -anse, -ence, -ense

waitress la serveuse
actress l'actrice
cooker (or female cook) la cuisinière
vegetarian (female) la végétarienne
rubbish bin la poubelle
festival, party la fête
shrimp la crevette
mustard la moutarde
sleeve la manche
size la taille
cupboard l'armoire
year l'année
beauty la beauté
friendship l'amitié
crown la couronne
reason la raison
(metro) station la station
caress la caresse
friend (female) l'amie
kitchen la cuisine
moon la lune
rate, speed l'allure
change (of train/bus) la correspondance
dance la danse
licence la license

need to know

Adding an -s to a word doesn't change its pronunciation.

Adjectives (pretty, tall)

Adjectives are 'describing' words that tell you more about a person or thing, such as colour or size. In French adjectives 'agree' with the noun they describe.

For the feminine singular form of the adjective, you usually add -e to the masculine singular, unless the adjective already ends with an -e (eg **jeune, pauvre**). For the masculine plural, you usually add -s to the masculine singular, unless the adjective already ends in an -s or an -x (eg **gros, heureux**); and for the feminine plural you usually add -es to the masculine singular (eg **grand/grandes**).

Most French adjectives go after the noun they describe, but some very common adjectives usually come before the noun: **bon, mauvais, court, long, grand, petit, gros, beau, joli, jeune, nouveau, vieux**.

In some cases there is a change of meaning involved depending on whether the adjective goes before or after the noun: **mon propre bureau** 'my own office' *but* **un bureau propre** 'a clean office' and **mon ancienne école** 'my old school' (former, previous) *but* **cette école est très ancienne** 'this school is very old' (ancient).

When an adjective comes before a plural noun, **des** changes to **de**: **j'ai reçu de beaux cadeaux** I got some lovely presents.

big	**grand(e)** *groñ(d)*	small	**petit(e)** *puh-tee(t)*	
beautiful	**beau/belle** *bo/bel*	ugly	**laid(e)** *lay(d)*	
fat	**gros(se)** *groh(s)*	thin	**mince** *mañss*	
long	**long(ue)** *loñ(g)*	short	**court(e)** *koor(t)*	
new	**nouveau/nouvelle** *noo-voh/noo-vel*	old	**vieux/vieille** *vyuh/vyay*	
good	**bon/bonne** *boñ/bon*	bad	**mauvais(e)** *moh-vay(-vez)*	
happy	**heureux/heureuse** *uh-ruh/uh-ruhz*	sad	**triste** *treest*	
rich	**riche** *reesh*	poor	**pauvre** *pohv-ruh*	

Possessives (my, mine, his)

Possessives (adjectives or pronouns) tell you who is connected with the thing referred to: 'my car', 'your horse'.

Here are the masculine, feminine and plural adjective and pronoun forms:

my	**mon/ma/mes**
mine, my one(s)	**le mien/la mienne/les miens/les miennes**
your (*informal singular*)	**ton/ta/tes**
yours, your one(s)	**le tien/la tienne/les tiens/les tiennes**
his/her/one's/its	**son/sa/ses**
his/hers, one's/its one(s)	**le sien/la sienne/les siens/les siennes**
our	**notre/notre/nos**
ours, our one(s)	**le nôtre/la nôtre/les nôtres**
your (*plural or formal singular*)	**votre/votre/vos**
yours, your one(s)	**le vôtre/la vôtre/les vôtres**
their	**leur/leur/leurs**
theirs, their one(s)	**le leur/la leur/les leurs**

> **need to know**
>
> Careful! don't go thinking that **son** means 'his' and **sa** means 'her'!

The choice of **son/sa** and **leur/leurs** depends on the thing or person 'owned', not the 'owner': **il adore sa voiture** he loves his car, **elle n'aime pas son travail** she doesn't like her work.

my keys, please	**mes clés, s'il vous plaît** *may klay, seel voo play*
these keys are mine	**ces clés sont les miennes** *say klay soñ lay myen*
that's our hotel	**voilà notre hôtel** *vwa-la notr oh-tel*
your hotel? yes, ours	**votre hôtel? oui, le nôtre** *votr oh-tel? wee, luh nohtr*
which passport is hers?	**quel passeport est le sien?** *kel pass-por ay luh syañ?*
they don't like their room	**ils n'aiment pas leur chambre** *eel nem pa luhr shoñ-bruh*

Demonstratives (this, that)

Words like 'this', 'that', 'these' and 'those' are a special kind of adjective, known as demonstrative adjectives. They point to a particular thing to distinguish it from others nearer or further off in space or time.

The words in French are **ce** (masculine) **cette** (feminine) and **ces** (plural). There is also **cet**, used before a masculine noun beginning with a vowel or most words beginning with **h-**. In terms of meanings these words cover both 'this' and 'that'.

Don't confuse this **ce** with the demonstrative pronoun used in expressions such as **c'est** and **ce sont** meaning 'it is', 'they are'. Other similar pronouns are **ceci** 'this', **cela** 'that' and **ça** less formal 'this' or 'that'.

If you need to make a difference between 'this' and 'that' you can add something to the end of the word to distinguish it: **-ci** for 'this' and **-là** for 'that'. It's a bit like saying 'this thing here' or 'that thing there'.

Here's the full pattern:

masculine singular	**celui-ci** this one	**celui-là** that one
feminine singular	**celle-ci** this one	**celle-là** that one
masculine plural	**ceux-ci** these ones	**ceux-là** those ones
feminine plural	**celles-ci** these ones	**celles-là** those ones

this month
ce mois
suh mwa

this time it's different
cette fois c'est différent
set fwa say dee-fay-roñ

I've never seen these/those boys
je n'ai jamais vu ces garçons
zhuh nay zha-may voo say gar-soñ

these boys (here) or those boys (there)?
ces garçons-ci ou ces garçons-là?
say gar-soñ-see oo say gar-soñ-la?

it doesn't matter
ça ne fait rien
sa nuh fay ryañ

give me that!
donne moi ça!
don mwa sa!

I'd like this one (here)
je voudrais celui-ci
zhuh voo-dray suh-lwee-see

Colours (red, yellow, blue)

Colours are adjectives and agree with the noun they are describing. Unlike in English, in French colours always follow the noun.

black	**noir(e)**	pink	**rose**	
	nwar		*roz*	
blue	**bleu(e)**	purple	**violet(te)**	
	bluh		*vyol-ay(-et)*	
brown	**marron**	red	**rouge**	
	ma-roñ		*roozh*	
green	**vert(e)**	white	**blanc/blanche**	
	vehr(t)		*bloñ/bloñsh*	
grey	**gris(e)**	yellow	**jaune**	
	gree(z)		*zhohn*	
orange	**orange**			
	o-roñzh			

However there are some colours which are 'invariable' and never change. These are often made up of more than one word – for example, **bleu marine** meaning 'navy blue', or else come from the names of fruit or nuts, for example, **orange** 'orange', **marron** 'brown': **une veste bleu marine** 'a navy blue jacket' and **des chaussures marron** 'brown shoes'.

what colour is it?	**c'est de quelle couleur?**
	say duh kel koo-luhr
a blue door	**une porte bleue**
	oon port bluh
white sheets	**des draps blancs**
	day dra bloñ
light/dark	**clair/foncé**
	klehr/foñ-say
a light blue shirt	**une chemise bleu clair**
	oon shuh-meez bluh klehr
a dark grey car	**une voiture gris foncé**
	oon vwa-toor gree foñ-say

Prepositions (in, on, at)

Prepositions usually tell us something to do with position or time: '*in* a small market', '*near* the centre of Manchester', '*at* 8 o'clock'. The only slight difficulty is that the choice of preposition is not always predictable. In English you travel 'on the train' but in French **dans le train** 'in the train', not **sur le train**, which would mean on top of it. 'In Manchester' is **à Manchester** 'at Manchester' rather than **dans Manchester** 'inside Manchester'.

Sometimes one language uses a preposition where it is not needed in the other, just as you can say either 'I wrote to my mother' or (in American English) 'I wrote my mother'. In French, 'look at my car' is just **regarde ma voiture**, but 'phone your mother' is **téléphone à ta mère**.

Some common prepositions:

à	to, at, in
de	of, from, about
dans	in, within, inside
sur	on
sous	under
entre	between
avant	before
après	after
vers	towards (with times, 'at about')
déjà	already
pour	for
avec	with
sans	without

When **le** and **les** are used after the prepositions **à** 'to', 'at' and **de** 'any', 'some', 'of', they contract as follows:

à + **le** = **au** (**au cinéma** but **à la gare**)

à + **les** = **aux** (**aux magasins** – applies to both masculine and feminine)

de + **le** = **du** (**du pain** but **de la confiture**)

de + **les** = **des** (**des pommes** – applies to both masculine and feminine)

to go to Paris	**aller à Paris**
	a-lay a pa-ree
a room at (=costing) €40	**une chambre à quarante euros**
	oon shoñ-bruh a ka-roñt uh-roh
in my opinion	**à mon avis**
	a moñn a-vee
my mother's childhood	**l'enfance de ma mère**
	loñ-foñss duh ma mehr
a letter from my sister	**une lettre de ma sœur**
	oon let-ruh duh ma suhr
from 5 to 10 euros	**de cinq à dix euros**
	duh sañk a deez uh-roh
in the street	**dans la rue**
	doñ la roo
at about 10 o'clock	**vers dix heures**
	ver deez uhr
between 6 o'clock and midnight	**entre six heures et minuit**
	oñ-truh seez uhr ay meen-wee

need to know

When pronouns come after prepositions they are the emphatic sort: à moi, pour vous.

Questions (when? where? how?)

There are a number of different ways of asking questions in French: using **est-ce que?**; or by turning verb and subject around (eg **avez-vous...?**); or by simply raising the pitch of your voice at the end of the phrase (**vous avez...?**). And just as in English, in French there are various words used in questions where the answer is not a simple yes or no. In English these words often begin with 'wh-': 'which', 'why', 'who' etc.

So, if the answer was **oui, j'aime bien la France** 'yes, I like France', the question might be **est-ce que vous aimez la France?** or **aimez-vous la France?** or **vous aimez la France?** The most straightforward and versatile of these methods is probably the last one. It's very common in everyday speech although it might seem a little too informal in written contexts. On the other hand, the 'inversion' method (**aimez-vous la France**), though quite common in writing, can seem too formal in conversation.

You can use all three of these methods with question words such as **quand** 'when', **qui** 'who', **quel** 'which', **où** 'where', **combien** 'how much/many' and **comment** 'how': **quand est-ce que vous arrivez?** or **quand arrivez-vous?** or **vous arrivez quand?**

Quel 'which...?' or 'what...?' applies to a noun 'which/what car?', while **lequel** replaces a noun 'which?', 'which one?. They each have masculine/feminine and singular/plural forms:

	masculine	feminine	
singular	**quel?**	**quelle?**	who?/what?/which?
plural	**quels?**	**quelles?**	who?/what?/which?
singular	**lequel?**	**laquelle?**	which? which one?
plural	**lesquels?**	**lesquelles?**	which ones?

> **need to know**
>
> When two vowels come together in an inverted question, for example va+il, a -t- is inserted to make it easier to say: comment va-t-il?

how much/many?	**combien?**
	koñb-yañ?
how?	**comment?**
	ko-moñ?

where?	où?
	oo?
why?	pourquoi?
	poor-kwa?
when?	quand?
	koñ?
who?	qui?
	kee?
what?	que?
	kuh?
how many apples?	combien de pommes?
	koñb-yañ duh pom
how much does this computer cost?	combien coûte cet ordinateur?
	koñb-yañ koot set or-dee-na-tuhr
how is she?	comment va-t-elle?
	koñ-moñ va-tel?
where are you going?	où allez-vous?
	oo a-lay voo?
why isn't he coming?	pourquoi est-ce qu'il ne vient pas?
	poor-kwa ess-keel nuh vyañ pa?
when are you leaving?	quand est-ce que tu pars?
	koñt ess kuh too par?
who is there?	qui est là?
	kee ay la?
what are you eating?	qu'est-ce que tu manges?
	kess kuh too mañzh?
who's your favourite singer?	quel est ton chanteur préféré?
	kel ay toñ shoñ-tuhr pray-fay-ray
which shoes do you like?	quelles chaussures te plaisent?
	kel shoh-soor tuh plez

need to know

Quelle chance! quel **sounds the same in all its forms. It's only when you are writing that you have to remember the endings!**

Negatives (no, not, never)

A negative question or statement is one where something is not happening, is not true, is not present: 'never', 'nobody', 'nothing'. In French, to make something negative, you generally use a pair of words, for example, **ne ... pas** with the verb in the middle.

ne ... pas	not
ne ... rien	nothing, not ... anything
ne ... personne	nobody, not ... anybody,
ne ... jamais	never, not ... ever
ne ... plus	no longer, no more

> **need to know**
>
> **Some of these negative words can be used on their own as well:**
> jamais! **'never!'** rien! **'nothing!'** personne! **'nobody!'**

After these types of negative expressions, **un(e)**, **du**, **de la**, **de l'** and **des** all change to **de** or **d'**, as follows. It may help you to replace these in your mind with 'no' in the English:

nous n'avons pas de beurre we haven't got any butter, we have no butter (not **du**)
elle n'a pas de voiture she hasn't got a car, she has no car (not **une**)
je ne mange pas de viande I don't eat meat, I eat no meat (not **de la**)
il n'y a plus de bus there aren't any more buses, there are no more buses (not **des**)

When a verb is in the infinitive, **ne ... pas**, **ne ... rien**, **ne ... plus** and **ne ... jamais** come together before the infinitive:

il essayait de ne pas rire he was trying not to laugh.

The word **pas** can be used on its own when a distinction is being made, or for emphasis, just like 'not' in English: **pas moi!** not me! or **pas encore** not yet.

I don't smoke	**je ne fume pas**
	zhuh nuh foom pa
don't change anything	**ne changez rien**
	nuh shoñ-zhay ryañ
I can't see anybody	**je ne vois personne**
	zhuh nuh vwa pehr-son
she never arrives on time	**elle n'arrive jamais à l'heure**
	el na-reev zha-may a luhr

17 Adverbs (slowly, fast)

An adverb describes a verb or an adjective: 'she walked slowly' and 'the car is very slow'. They can also refer to a whole idea or sentence: 'maybe he's on holiday' and 'she always thinks she's right, but often she's wrong'. In English they typically end '-ly': 'slowly', 'luckily', etc. In French the most common ending is **-ment**.

To form an adverb in French, you take the feminine form of the adjective (eg for 'slow' **lente**, from **lent**, or **heureuse** from **heureux**, 'happy') and add **-ment**: **lentement**, **heureusement** 'slowly', 'happily'. Some are slightly irregular, for example adverbs coming from adjectives ending in **-ent** or **-ant** (eg **brillant** 'brilliant', **récent** 'recent') take the endings **-emment** and **-amment**: **brillamment** 'brilliantly', and **récemment** 'recently'. Many adverbs are completely different and do not obey this rule at all. Here are some examples:

fast, quickly	**vite**
	veet
well	**bien**
	byañ
badly	**mal**
	mal
often	**souvent**
	soo-voñ
soon	**bientôt**
	byañ-toh
yet	**encore**
	oñ-kor
already	**déjà**
	day-zha
now	**maintenant**
	mañ-tuh-noñ
always	**toujours**
	too-zhoor

need to know

To form an adverb in French, generally you need to find the feminine form of the adjective to start with.

Pronouns (I, me, he)

Pronouns are really a special type of noun, used to stand in for another noun so as to avoid repeating it every time you refer to the same thing or person 'Mary works in a shop ... Mary sells vegetables'. You can use a pronoun and change the second 'Mary' to '*she* sells vegetables'. The same thing happens in French, Mary becomes **elle** 'she'.

The only real complication is that French has two words for 'you' (**tu** and **vous**) where English gets by with one – unless you count the word 'yous' that you sometimes hear nowadays. The word **vous** is used for more than one person, or for a single person in more polite or formal situations, while **tu** is for people you know well, children or animals.

These are the pronouns used for the subject of a sentence (the one who performs the action).

je	I
tu	you (informal singular)
il	he/it
elle	she/it
on	(impersonal: one, you, we, 'people')
nous	we
vous	you (plural or formal singular)
ils	they (masculine or mixed)
elles	they (exclusively female)

> **need to know**
>
> **With a mixed-gender group of things or people, males take precedence! Use the masculine pronoun.**

There is a different set of pronouns for the object of the sentence. But what about when a sentence has two objects, for example 'him' and 'it' in 'I bought him it'? Well, one of these pronouns is more central to the sentence than the other, since you can say 'I bought it' with the same meaning, whereas 'I bought him' means something different. So 'it' is the 'direct' object here, and 'him' indirect. You can usually tell which is the indirect pronoun by putting 'for' or 'to' in front of it: 'I bought him it' – 'I bought it for him'. The point of this distinction is that different words are needed in French for these two sorts of pronoun. The differences are: **lui** (indirect for 'him' and 'her') instead of **le**, and **leur** (indirect for 'them', both masculine and feminine) instead of **les**.

Another type of pronoun is the emphatic pronoun, used in French after a preposition ('for you', 'towards me' etc), and when you want to emphasise something ('me?', 'it was you!'). They can also be used on their own without a verb.

direct	indirect	emphatic	
me/m'	me/m'	moi	me
te/t'	te/t'	toi	you
le/l'	lui	lui	him/it
la/l'	lui	elle	her/it
–	–	soi	impersonal **on**
nous	nous	nous	us
vous	vous	vous	you
les	leur	eux	them
les	leur	elles	them

Tom doesn't drink wine, he doesn't like it

Tom ne boit pas de vin, il n'aime pas ça
tom nuh bwa pa duh vañ, eel nem pa sa

Ann's very sporty, she loves football

Ann est très sportive, elle adore le football
an ay tray spor-teev, el a-dor luh foot-bol

Ann and Tom are not here, they are ill

Ann et Tom ne sont pas ici, ils sont malades
an ay tom nuh soñ paz ee-see, eel soñ ma-lad

Ann likes this soap, but Tom never watches it

Ann aime ce feuilleton, mais Tom ne le regarde jamais
an em suh fuh-yuh-toñ, may tom nuh luh ruh-gard zha-may

Tom doesn't like football, but Ann loves it

Tom n'aime pas le football, mais Ann l'adore
tom nem pa luh foot-bol, may an la-dor

I wrote to them

je leur ai écrit
zhuh luhr ay ay-kree

I spoke to them

je leur ai parlé
zhuh luhr ay par-lay

is that you, Simon?

c'est toi, Simon?
say twa, see-moñ?

come with me

venez avec moi
vuh-nay a-vek mwa

me too!

moi aussi!
mwa oh-see

Verbs (to be, to see, to do)

Verbs are the words that correspond to the action of a sentence. You may have heard them called 'doing words' at school. The ending of the verb varies according to who is doing the action (in English 'I go' but 'he goes'), and when the action happens ('I go' but 'I went').

The form in which you would look up a verb in the dictionary is known as the infinitive, meaning that it tells you nothing about who or when, just like 'to go' or 'to sing' in English. In French the infinitive is a single word: **aller**, **chanter**.

French verbs are grouped into three main categories according to the ending of that infinitive form, which in the vast majority of cases is either **-er**, **-re** or **-ir** (known as 'regular verbs'). Of course there are various 'irregular verbs' as well. As in English, some of the most important verbs are irregular: 'to be' **être**, 'to go' **aller**.

The different forms of the verb reflecting time are called tenses: present, future, etc. There are different kinds of past tense: one called the perfect tense tells you about a single complete action that is finished and done with, while the imperfect tense denotes an action that continues over a period of time or was still ongoing when something else happened. We have something similar in English with 'I had a shower and went out' as opposed to 'I was having a shower when the phone rang'. The perfect can also be translated using 'have': 'I have had a shower', 'I have never been to Italy'.

The imperative (command) is the form you use to give orders to others 'do this!' or make suggestions involving a group including yourself 'let's do this!'. We've given the forms corresponding to **tu**, **nous** and **vous** in that order: **mange!** 'eat!', (informal singular), **mangeons!** 'let's eat' and **mangez!** 'eat!' (formal or plural).

The subjunctive is used in constructions involving an unreal or hypothetical case, and in so-called indirect commands, especially following the word **que** 'that, for example in **je veux que tu le fasses** 'I want you to do it', literally 'I want that you should do it'.

We give examples of each of the regular verbs and a selection of important irregular ones. There is also an example of each tense given to show it in use.

arriver (-er verb, to arrive)

Present	j'	arrive *a-reev*	the train arrives at 5.34pm
	tu	arrives *a-reev*	le train **arrive** à 17 heures 34
	il/elle/on	arrive *a-reev*	*luh trañ a-reev a dee-set uhr troñt-katr*
	nous	arrivons *a-ree-voñ*	
	vous	arrivez *a-ree-vay*	
	ils/elles	arrivent *a-reev*	
Future	j'	arriverai *a-reev-ray*	we'll arrive in the evening
	tu	arriveras *a-reev-ra*	nous **arriverons** dans la soirée
	il/elle/on	arrivera *a-reev-ra*	*nooz a-reev-roñ doñ la swa-ray*
	nous	arriverons *a-reev-roñ*	
	vous	arriverez *a-reev-ray*	
	ils/elles	arriveront *a-reev-roñ*	
Past: perfect	je	suis arrivé(e) *sweez a-ree-vay*	he arrived twenty minutes late
	tu	es arrivé(e) *ayz a-ree-vay*	il **est arrivé** avec vingt minutes de retard
	il/elle/on	est arrivé(e) *ayt a-ree-vay*	*eel ayt a-ree-vay a-vek vañ mee-noot duh ruh-tar*
	nous	sommes arrivé(e)s *somz a-ree-vay*	
	vous	êtes arrivé(e)(s) *etz a-ree-vay*	
	ils/elles	sont arrivé(e)s *soñt a-ree-vay*	
Past: imperfect	j'	arrivais *a-ree-vay*	she couldn't shut the door
	tu	arrivais *a-ree-vay*	elle n'**arrivait** pas à fermer la porte
	il/elle/on	arrivait *a-ree-vay*	*el na-ree-vay paz a fehr-may la port*
	nous	arrivions *a-reev-yoñ*	
	vous	arriviez *a-reev-yay*	
	ils/elles	arrivaient *a-ree-vay*	
Conditional	j'	arriverais *a-reev-ray*	you would get there sooner if you took
	tu	arriverais *a-reev-ray*	the plane
	il/elle/on	arriverait *a-reev-ray*	tu **arriverais** plus tôt si tu prenais l'avion
	nous	arriverions *a-ree-vuhr-ryoñ*	*too a-reev-ray ploo toh see too pruh-nay lav-yoñ*
	vous	arriveriez *a-ree-vuhr-yay*	
	ils/elles	arriveraient *a-reev-ray*	
Subjunctive	j'	arrive *a-reev*	you must arrive at least an hour before
	tu	arrives *a-reev*	boarding
	il/elle/on	arrive *a-reev*	il faut que vous **arriviez** au moins une
	nous	arrivions *a-reev-yoñ*	heure avant l'embarquement
	vous	arriviez *a-reev-yay*	*eel foh kuh vooz a-reev-yay oh mwañ oon uhr*
	ils/elles	arrivent *a-reev*	*a-voñ loñ-bar-kuh-moñ*
Imperative		arrive! *a-reev!*	
(command)		arrivons! *a-ree-voñ!*	
		arrivez! *a-ree-vay!*	

répondre (-re verb, to reply)

21

Present	je	**réponds** *ray-poñ*	I tried to to call but there's no answer
	tu	**réponds** *ray-poñ*	j'ai essayé d'appeler mais ça ne **répond** pas
	il/elle/on	**répond** *ray-poñ*	*zhay e-say-yay dap-lay may sa nuh ray-poñ pa*
	nous	**répondons** *ray-poñ-doñ*	
	vous	**répondez** *ray-poñ-day*	
	ils/elles	**répondent** *ray-poñd*	
Future	je	**répondrai** *ray-poñ-dray*	will you reply to him or shall I?
	tu	**répondras** *ray-poñ-dra*	tu lui **répondras** ou tu veux que je le fasse?
	il/elle/on	**répondra** *ray-poñ-dra*	*too lwee ray-poñ-dra oo too vuh kuh zhuh luh fass?*
	nous	**répondrons** *ray-poñ-droñ*	
	vous	**répondrez** *ray-poñ-dray*	
	ils/elles	**répondront** *ray-poñ-droñ*	
Past: perfect	j'	**ai répondu** *ay ray-poñ-doo*	did she reply to your e-mail?
	tu	**as répondu** *a ray-poñ-doo*	est-ce qu'elle **a répondu** à ton mail?
	il/elle/on	**a répondu** *a ray-poñ-doo*	*ess kel a ray-poñ-doo a toñ mel?*
	nous	**avons répondu** *a-voñ ray-poñ-doo*	
	vous	**avez répondu** *a-vay ray-poñ-doo*	
	ils/elles	**ont répondu** *oñ ray-poñ-doo*	
Past: imperfect	je	**répondais** *ray-poñ-day*	he didn't reply to any questions
	tu	**répondais** *ray-poñ-day*	il ne **répondait** à aucune question
	il/elle/on	**répondait** *ray-poñ-day*	*eel nuh ray-poñ-dayt a oh-koon kest-yoñ*
	nous	**répondions** *ray-poñd-yoñ*	
	vous	**répondiez** *ray-poñd-yay*	
	ils/elles	**répondaient** *ray-poñ-day*	
Conditional	je	**répondrais** *ray-poñ-dray*	I thought you would reply to him
	tu	**répondrais** *ray-poñ-dray*	j'ai pensé que tu lui **répondrais**
	il/elle/on	**répondrait** *ray-poñ-dray*	*zhay poñ-say kuh too lwee ray-poñ-dray*
	nous	**répondrions** *ray-poñd-ree-yoñ*	
	vous	**répondriez** *ray-poñd-ree-yay*	
	ils/elles	**répondraient** *ray-poñd-ray*	
Subjunctive	je	**réponde** *ray-poñd*	I'd like you to answer me
	tu	**répondes** *ray-poñd*	j'aimerais bien que tu me **répondes**
	il/elle/on	**réponde** *ray-poñd*	*zhaym-ray byañ kuh too muh ray-poñd*
	nous	**répondions** *ray-poñd-yoñ*	
	vous	**répondiez** *ray-poñd-yay*	
	ils/elles	**répondent** *ray-poñd*	
Imperative		**réponds!** *ray-poñ!*	
(command)		**répondons!** *ray-poñ-doñ!*	
		répondez! *ray-poñ-day!*	

finir (-ir verb, to finish)

Present	je	**finis** *fee-nee*	what time does the film finish?
	tu	**finis** *fee-nee*	le film **finit** à quelle heure?
	il/elle/on	**finit** *fee-nee*	*luh feelm fee-nee a kel uhr?*
	nous	**finissons** *fee-nee-soñ*	
	vous	**finissez** *fee-nee-say*	
	ils/elles	**finissent** *fee-neess*	
Future	je	**finirai** *fee-nee-ray*	come on, you'll finish later
	tu	**finiras** *fee-nee-ra*	viens! Tu **finiras** plus tard
	il/elle/on	**finira** *fee-nee-ra*	*vyañ! too fee-nee-ra ploo tar*
	nous	**finirons** *fee-nee-roñ*	
	vous	**finirez** *fee-nee-ray*	
	ils/elles	**finiront** *fee-nee-roñ*	
Past: perfect	j'	**ai fini** *ay fee-nee*	Mark hasn't finished his homework yet
	tu	**as fini** *a fee-nee*	Marc n'**a** pas encore **fini** ses devoirs
	il/elle/on	**a fini** *a fee-nee*	*mark na paz oñ-kor fee-nee say duh-vwar*
	nous	**avons fini** *a-voñ fee-nee*	
	vous	**avez fini** *a-vay fee-nee*	
	ils/elles	**ont fini** *oñ fee-nee*	
Past: imperfect	je	**finissais** *fee-nee-say*	they had just finished eating when I arrived
	tu	**finissais** *fee-nee-say*	ils **finissaient** à peine de manger quand je
	il/elle/on	**finissait** *fee-nee-say*	suis arrivé
	nous	**finissions** *fee-neess-yoñ*	*eel fee-nee-sayt a pen duh moñ-zhay koñ zhuh*
	vous	**finissiez** *fee-neess-yay*	*sweez a-ree-vay*
	ils/elles	**finissaient** *fee-nee-say*	
Conditional	je	**finirais** *fee-nee-ray*	you said you'd finish repainting the living
	tu	**finirais** *fee-nee-ray*	room before Christmas
	il/elle/on	**finirait** *fee-nee-ray*	tu m'avais dit que tu **finirais** de repeindre le
	nous	**finirions** *fee-neer-yoñ*	salon avant Noël
	vous	**finiriez** *fee-neer-yay*	*too ma-vay dee kuh too fee-nee-ray duh*
	ils/elles	**finiraient** *fee-nee-ray*	*ruh-pañ-druh luh sa-loñ a-voñ noh-el*
Subjunctive	je	**finisse** *fee-neess*	I must finish writing my postcards today
	tu	**finisses** *fee-neess*	il faut que je **finisse** d'écrire mes cartes
	il/elle/on	**finisse** *fee-neess*	postales aujourd'hui
	nous	**finissions** *fee-neess-yoñ*	*eel foh kuh zhuh fee-neess day-kreer may kart*
	vous	**finissiez** *fee-neess-yay*	*po-stal oh-zhoor-dwee*
	ils/elles	**finissent** *fee-neess*	
Imperative		**finis!** *fee-nee!*	
(command)		**finissons!** *fee-nee-soñ!*	
		finissez! *fee-nee-say!*	

être (to be)

Present			
	je	**suis** *swee*	
	tu	**es** *ay*	
	il/elle/on	**est** *ay*	
	nous	**sommes** *som*	
	vous	**êtes** *et*	
	ils/elles	**sont** *soñ*	

Paris is a very beautiful city
Paris **est** une très belle ville
pa-ree ayt oon tray bel veel

Future		
	je	**serai** *suh-ray*
	tu	**seras** *suh-ra*
	il/elle/on	**sera** *suh-ra*
	nous	**serons** *suh-roñ*
	vous	**serez** *suh-ray*
	ils/elles	**seront** *suh-roñ*

the weather will be sunny throughout the
south of the country
le temps **sera** ensoleillé dans tout le sud
du pays
luh toñ suh-rah oñ-so-lay-yay doñ too luh sood doo pay

Past: perfect		
	j'	**ai été** *ay ay-tay*
	tu	**as été** *a ay-tay*
	il/elle/on	**a été** *a ay-tay*
	nous	**avons été** *a-voñ zay-tay*
	vous	**avez été** *a-vayz ay-tay*
	ils/elles	**ont été** *oñt ay-tay*

I was a little disappointed by the trip
j'**ai été** un peu déçu par le voyage
zhay ay-tay uhñ puh day-soo par luh vwa-yazh

Past: imperfect		
	j'	**étais** *ay-tay*
	tu	**étais** *ay-tay*
	il/elle/on	**était** *ay-tay*
	nous	**étions** *ayt-yoñ*
	vous	**étiez** *ayt-yay*
	ils/elles	**étaient** *ayt-ay*

the meal was delicious
le repas **était** délicieux
luh ruh-pa ay-tay day-leess-yuh

Conditional		
	je	**serais** *suh-ray*
	tu	**serais** *suh-ray*
	il/elle/on	**serait** *suh-ray*
	nous	**serions** *suhr-yoñ*
	vous	**seriez** *suhr-yay*
	ils/elles	**seraient** *suh-ray*

you'd be more comfortable in this chair
tu **serais** plus à l'aise dans ce fauteuil
too suh-ray plooz a lehz doñ suh foh-tuhy

Subjunctive		
	je	**sois** *swa*
	tu	**sois** *swa*
	il/elle/on	**soit** *swa*
	nous	**soyons** *swa-yoñ*
	vous	**soyez** *swa-ay*
	ils/elles	**soient** *swa*

I don't think she's there
je ne crois pas qu'elle **soit** là
zhuh nuh krwa pa kel swa la

Imperative (command)	
	sois! *swa!*
	soyons! *swa-yoñ!*
	soyez! *swa-yay!*

avoir (to have)

Present	j'	**ai** *ay*		do you have a bus timetable?
	tu	**as** *a*		vous **avez** l'horaire des bus?
	il/elle/on	**a** *a*		*vooz a-vay lo-rehr day boos?*
	nous	**avons** *a-voñ*		
	vous	**avez** *a-vay*		
	ils/elles	**ont** *oñ*		
Future	j'	**aurai** *o-ray*		she will be five next month
	tu	**auras** *o-ra*		elle **aura** cinq ans le mois prochain
	il/elle/on	**aura** *o-ra*		*el o-ra sañk oñ luh mwa pro-shañ*
	nous	**aurons** *o-roñ*		
	vous	**aurez** *o-ray*		
	ils/elles	**auront** *o-roñ*		
Past: perfect	j'	**ai eu** *ay oo*		I had a headache all evening
	tu	**as eu** *a oo*		j'**ai eu** mal à la tête toute la soirée
	il/elle/on	**a eu** *a oo*		*zhay oo mal a la tet toot la swa-ray*
	nous	**avons eu** *a-voñz oo*		
	vous	**avez eu** *a-vayz oo*		
	ils/elles	**ont eu** *oñt oo*		
Past: imperfect	j'	**avais** *a-vay*		there was no more room on the train
	tu	**avais** *a-vay*		il n'y **avait** plus de place dans le train
	il/elle/on	**avait** *a-vay*		*eel nee a-vay ploo duh plass doñ luh trañ*
	nous	**avions** *av-yoñ*		
	vous	**aviez** *av-yay*		
	ils/elles	**avaient** *a-vay*		
Conditional	j'	**aurais** *o-ray*		would you have time to do it tomorrow?
	tu	**aurais** *o-ray*		tu **aurais** le temps de le faire demain?
	il/elle/on	**aurait** *o-ray*		*too o-ray luh toñ duh luh fehr duh-mañ?*
	nous	**aurions** *or-yoñ*		
	vous	**auriez** *or-yay*		
	ils/elles	**auraient** *o-ray*		
Subjunctive	j'	**aie** *ay*		take off the blanket so she isn't too hot
	tu	**aies** *ay*		retire la couverture pour qu'elle n'**ait** pas
	il/elle/on	**ait** *ay*		trop chaud
	nous	**ayons** *ay-yoñ*		*ruh-teer la koo-vehr-toor poor kel nay pa troh shoh*
	vous	**ayez** *ay-yay*		
	ils/elles	**aient** *ay*		
Imperative		**aie!** *ay!*		
(command)		**ayons!** *ay-yoñ!*		
		ayez! *a-yay!*		

aller (to go)

25

Present	je	**vais** *vay*	I'm going to Lyon for a meeting je **vais** à Lyon pour une réunion *zhuh vayz a lyoñ poor oon ray-oon-yoñ*
	tu	**vas** *va*	
	il/elle/on	**va** *va*	
	nous	**allons** *a-loñ*	
	vous	**allez** *a-lay*	
	ils/elles	**vont** *voñ*	
Future	j'	**irai** *ee-ray*	we'll go to see Granny tomorrow nous **irons** voir mamie demain *nooz ee-roñ vwar ma-mee duh-mañ*
	tu	**iras** *ee-ra*	
	il/elle/on	**ira** *ee-ra*	
	nous	**irons** *ee-roñ*	
	vous	**irez** *ee-ray*	
	ils/elles	**iront** *ee-roñ*	
Past: perfect	je	**suis allé(e)** *sweez a-lay*	they went on holiday to Sicily ils **sont allés** en vacances en Sicile *eel soñt a-lay oñ va-koñss oñ see-seel*
	tu	**es allé(e)** *ayz a-lay*	
	il/elle/on	**est allé(e)** *ayt a-lay*	
	nous	**sommes allé(e)s** *somz a-lay*	
	vous	**êtes allé(e)(s)** *etz a-lay*	
	ils/elles	**sont allé(e)s** *soñt a-lay*	
Past: imperfect	j'	**allais** *a-lay*	she was going to a concert elle **allait** à un concert *el a-layt a uñ koñ-sehr*
	tu	**allais** *a-lay*	
	il/elle/on	**allait** *a-lay*	
	nous	**allions** *al-yoñ*	
	vous	**alliez** *al-yay*	
	ils/elles	**allaient** *a-lay*	
Conditional	j'	**irais** *ee-ray*	if we lived in this part of town, that's where he would go to school si on habitait dans ce quartier, c'est là qu'il **irait** à l'école *see oñn a-bee-tay doñ suh kart-yay, say la keel ee-rayt a lay-kol*
	tu	**irais** *ee-ray*	
	il/elle/on	**irait** *ee-ray*	
	nous	**irions** *eer-yoñ*	
	vous	**iriez** *eer-yay*	
	ils/elles	**iraient** *eer-ay*	
Subjunctive	j'	**aille** *aee*	I don't want you to go too far je ne veux pas que tu **ailles** trop loin *zhuh nuh vuh pa kuh too aee troh lwañ*
	tu	**ailles** *aee*	
	il/elle/on	**aille** *aee*	
	nous	**allions** *al-yoñ*	
	vous	**alliez** *al-yay*	
	ils/elles	**aillent** *aee*	
Imperative *(command)*		**va!** *va!* **allons!** *a-loñ!* **allez!** *a-lay!*	

devoir (to have to)

Present	je	**dois** *dwa*		I have to leave early tomorrow morning
	tu	**dois** *dwa*		je **dois** partir de bonne heure demain matin
	il/elle/on	**doit** *dwa*		*zhuh dwa par-teer duh bon uhr duh-mañ ma-tañ*
	nous	**devons** *duh-voñ*		
	vous	**devez** *duh-vay*		
	ils/elles	**doivent** *dwav*		

Future	je	**devrai** *duh-vray*		they will have to spend the night at the airport
	tu	**devras** *duh-vra*		ils **devront** passer la nuit à l'aéroport
	il/elle/on	**devra** *duh-vra*		*eel dev-roñ pa-say la nwee a la-ay-ro-por*
	nous	**devrons** *duh-vroñ*		
	vous	**devrez** *duh-vray*		
	ils/elles	**devront** *duh-vroñ*		

Past: perfect	j'	**ai dû** *ay doo*		she had to take the next train
	tu	**as dû** *a doo*		elle **a dû** prendre le train suivant
	il/elle/on	**a dû** *a doo*		*el a doo proñd-ruh luh trañ swee-voñ*
	nous	**avons dû** *a-voñ doo*		
	vous	**avez dû** *a-vay doo*		
	ils/elles	**ont dû** *oñ doo*		

Past: imperfect	je	**devais** *duh-vay*		we were supposed to meet them at the
	tu	**devais** *duh-vay*		restaurant
	il/elle/on	**devait** *duh-vay*		nous **devions** les retrouver au restaurant
	nous	**devions** *duhv-yoñ*		*noo duhv-yoñ lay ruh-troo-vay oh rest-o-roñ*
	vous	**deviez** *duhv-yay*		
	ils/elles	**devaient** *duh-vay*		

Conditional	je	**devrais** *duhv-ray*		you should phone him
	tu	**devrais** *duhv-ray*		tu **devrais** lui téléphoner
	il/elle/on	**devrait** *duhv-ray*		*too duhv-ray lwee tay-lay-fo-nay*
	nous	**devrions** *duhv-ree-yoñ*		
	vous	**devriez** *duhv-ree-yay*		
	ils/elles	**devraient** *duhv-ray*		

Subjunctive	je	**doive** *dwav*		it's possible we'll have to pay a supplement
	tu	**doives** *dwav*		il est possible que nous **devions** payer un
	il/elle/on	**doive** *dwav*		supplément
	nous	**devions** *duhv-yoñ*		*eel ay po-seebl kuh noo duhv-yoñ pay-yay uñ*
	vous	**deviez** *duhv-yay*		*soo-play-moñ*
	ils/elles	**doivent** *dwav*		

Imperative	**dois!** *dwa!*	
(command)	**devons!** *duh-voñ!*	
	devez! *duh-vay!*	

faire (to make, to do)

Present			
	je	**fais** *fay*	she does her shopping at the market
	tu	**fais** *fay*	elle **fait** ses courses au marché
	il/elle/on	**fait** *fay*	*el fay say koorss oh mar-shay*
	nous	**faisons** *fuh-zoñ*	
	vous	**faites** *fet*	
	ils/elles	**font** *foñ*	

Future			
	je	**ferai** *fuh-ray*	it will be very cold in central France
	tu	**feras** *fuh-ra*	il **fera** très froid dans le centre de la France
	il/elle/on	**fera** *fuh-ra*	*eel fuh-ra tray frwa doñ luh soñ-truh duh la froñss*
	nous	**ferons** *fuh-roñ*	
	vous	**ferez** *fuh-ray*	
	ils/elles	**feront** *fuh-roñ*	

Past: perfect			
	j'	**ai fait** *ay fay*	what have you done today?
	tu	**as fait** *a fay*	qu'est-ce que vous **avez fait** aujourd'hui?
	il/elle/on	**a fait** *a fay*	*kess kuh vooz a-vay fay o-zhoor-dwee?*
	nous	**avons fait** *a-voñ fay*	
	vous	**avez fait** *a-vay fay*	
	ils/elles	**ont fait** *oñ fay*	

Past: imperfect			
	je	**faisais** *fuh-zay*	the weather was wonderful
	tu	**faisais** *fuh-zay*	il **faisait** un temps superbe
	il/elle/on	**faisait** *fuh-zay*	*eel fuh-zayt uñ toñ soo-pehrb*
	nous	**faisions** *fuh-zyoñ*	
	vous	**faisiez** *fuhz-yay*	
	ils/elles	**faisaient** *fuh-zay*	

Conditional			
	je	**ferais** *fuh-ray*	you would do better not to go there
	tu	**ferais** *fuh-ray*	tu **ferais** mieux de ne pas y aller
	il/elle/on	**ferait** *fuh-ray*	*too fuh-ray myuh duh nuh paz ee a-lay*
	nous	**ferions** *fuhr-yoñ*	
	vous	**feriez** *fuhr-yay*	
	ils/elles	**feraient** *fuh-ray*	

Subjunctive			
	je	**fasse** *fas*	you must be careful not to get lost
	tu	**fasses** *fas*	il faut que vous **fassiez** attention à ne pas
	il/elle/on	**fasse** *fas*	vous perdre
	nous	**fassions** *fas-yoñ*	*eel foh kuh voo fass-yay a-toñss-yoñ a nuh pa voo*
	vous	**fassiez** *fas-yay*	*pehr-druh*
	ils/elles	**fassent** *fas*	

Imperative		
(command)	**fais!** *fay*	
	faisons! *fuh-zoñ!*	
	faites! *fet!*	

vouloir (to want)

Present	je	**veux** *vuh*	I don't want any pudding
	tu	**veux** *vuh*	je ne **veux** pas de dessert
	il/elle/on	**veut** *vuh*	*zhuh nuh vuh pa duh day-sehr*
	nous	**voulons** *voo-loñ*	
	vous	**voulez** *voo-lay*	
	ils/elles	**veulent** *vuhl*	
Future	je	**voudrai** *voo-dray*	she will probably want to see you
	tu	**voudras** *voo-dra*	elle **voudra** sûrement te voir
	il/elle/on	**voudra** *voo-dra*	*el voo-dra soor-moñ tuh vwar*
	nous	**voudrons** *voo-droñ*	
	vous	**voudrez** *voo-dray*	
	ils/elles	**voudront** *voo-droñ*	
Past: perfect	j'	**ai voulu** *ay voo-loo*	they wouldn't stay
	tu	**as voulu** *a voo-loo*	ils n'**ont** pas **voulu** rester
	il/elle/on	**a voulu** *a voo-loo*	*eel noñ pa voo-loo res-tay*
	nous	**avons voulu** *a-voñ voo-loo*	
	vous	**avez voulu** *a-vay voo-loo*	
	ils/elles	**ont voulu** *oñ voo-loo*	
Past: imperfect	je	**voulais** *voo-lay*	she didn't want to go there
	tu	**voulais** *voo-lay*	elle ne **voulait** pas y aller
	il/elle/on	**voulait** *voo-lay*	*el nuh voo-lay paz ee a-lay*
	nous	**voulions** *vool-yoñ*	
	vous	**vouliez** *vool-yay*	
	ils/elles	**voulaient** *voo-lay*	
Conditional	je	**voudrais** *voo-dray*	I'd like five slices of ham
	tu	**voudrais** *voo-dray*	je **voudrais** cinq tranches de jambon
	il/elle/on	**voudrait** *voo-dray*	*zhuh voo-dray sañk troñsh duh zhoñ-boñ*
	nous	**voudrions** *vood-ree-yoñ*	
	vous	**voudriez** *vood-ree-yay*	
	ils/elles	**voudraient** *voo-dray*	
Subjunctive	je	**veuille** *vuhy*	we could go to the cinema, unless you would
	tu	**veuilles** *vuhy*	like to do something else
	il/elle/on	**veuille** *vuhy*	on pourrait aller au cinéma, à moins que tu
	nous	**voulions** *vool-yoñ*	ne **veuilles** faire autre chose
	vous	**vouliez** *vool-yay*	*oñ poo-ray a-lay oh see-nay-ma, a mwañ kuh too*
	ils/elles	**veuillent** *vuhy*	*nuh vuhy fehr oh-truh shohz*
Imperative		**veuille!** *vuhy!*	
(command)		**veuillons!** *vuh-yoñ!*	
		veuillez! *vuh-yay!*	

pouvoir (to be able)

Present			
	je	**peux** *puh*	can we have the bill?
	tu	**peux** *puh*	on **peut** avoir l'addition?
	il/elle/on	**peut** *puh*	*oñ puh a-vwar la-deess-yoñ*
	nous	**pouvons** *poo-voñ*	
	vous	**pouvez** *poo-vay*	
	ils/elles	**peuvent** *puhv*	

Future			
	je	**pourrai** *poo-ray*	can you wake me at seven o'clock?
	tu	**pourras** *poo-ra*	vous **pourrez** me réveiller à sept heures?
	il/elle/on	**pourra** *poo-ra*	*voo poo-ray muh ray-vay-yay a set uhr*
	nous	**pourrons** *poo-roñ*	
	vous	**pourrez** *poo-ray*	
	ils/elles	**pourront** *poo-roñ*	

Past: perfect			
	j'	**ai pu** *ay poo*	we weren't able to visit the Louvre
	tu	**as pu** *a poo*	on n'**a** pas **pu** visiter le Louvre
	il/elle/on	**a pu** *a poo*	*oñ na pa poo vee-zee-tay luh loovr*
	nous	**avons pu** *a-voñ poo*	
	vous	**avez pu** *a-vay poo*	
	ils/elles	**ont pu** *oñ poo*	

Past: imperfect			
	je	**pouvais** *poo-vay*	I couldn't phone you
	tu	**pouvais** *poo-vay*	je ne **pouvais** pas te téléphoner
	il/elle/on	**pouvait** *poo-vay*	*zhuh nuh poo-vay pa tuh tay-lay-fo-nay*
	nous	**pouvions** *poov-yoñ*	
	vous	**pouviez** *poov-yay*	
	ils/elles	**pouvaient** *poo-vay*	

Conditional			
	je	**pourrais** *poo-ray*	you could make an effort
	tu	**pourrais** *poo-ray*	tu **pourrais** faire un effort
	il/elle/on	**pourrait** *poo-ray*	*too poo-ray fehr uñn e-for*
	nous	**pourrions** *poor-yoñ*	
	vous	**pourriez** *poor-yay*	
	ils/elles	**pourraient** *poo-ray*	

Subjunctive			
	je	**puisse** *pweess*	it's the least I can do
	tu	**puisses** *pweess*	c'est le moins que je **puisse** faire
	il/elle/on	**puisse** *pweess*	*say luh mwañ kuh zhuh pweess fehr*
	nous	**puissions** *pweess-yoñ*	
	vous	**puissiez** *pweess-yay*	
	ils/elles	**puissent** *pweess*	

venir (to come)

Present			
je	**viens** *vyañ*		are you coming?
tu	**viens** *vyañ*		vous **venez**?
il/elle/on	**vient** *vyañ*		*voo vuh-nay?*
nous	**venons** *vuh-noñ*		
vous	**venez** *vuh-nay*		
ils/elles	**viennent** *vyen*		

Future			
je	**viendrai** *vyañ-dray*		Will you come to see us next summer?
tu	**viendras** *vyañ-dra*		vous **viendrez** nous voir l'été prochain?
il/elle/on	**viendra** *vyañ-dra*		*voo vyañ-dray noo vwar lay-tay pro-shañ?*
nous	**viendrons** *vyañ-droñ*		
vous	**viendrez** *vyañ-dray*		
ils/elles	**viendront** *vyañ-droñ*		

Past: perfect			
je	**suis venu(e)** *swee vuh-noo*		she didn't come
tu	**es venu(e)** *ay vuh-noo*		elle n'**est** pas **venue**
il/elle/on	**est venu(e)** *ay vuh-noo*		*el nay pa vuh-noo*
nous	**sommes venu(e)s** *som vuh-noo*		
vous	**êtes venu(e)(s)** *et vuh-noo*		
ils/elles	**sont venu(e)s** *soñ vuh-noo*		

Past: imperfect			
je	**venais** *vuh-nay*		his parents came from Algeria
tu	**venais** *vuh-nay*		ses parents **venaient** d'Algérie
il/elle/on	**venait** *vuh-nay*		*say pa-roñ vuh-nay dal-zhay-ree*
nous	**venions** *vuhn-yoñ*		
vous	**veniez** *vuhn-yay*		
ils/elles	**venaient** *vuh-nay*		

Conditional			
je	**viendrais** *vyañ-dray*		do you think he'd come if he was asked?
tu	**viendrais** *vyañ-dray*		tu crois qu'il **viendrait** si on lui demandait?
il/elle/on	**viendrait** *vyañ-dray*		*too krwa keel vyañ-dray see oñ lwee duh-moñ-day?*
nous	**viendrions** *vyañ-dree-yoñ*		
vous	**viendriez** *vyañ-dree-yay*		
ils/elles	**viendraient** *vyañ-dray*		

Subjunctive			
je	**vienne** *vyen*		do you want me to come with you?
tu	**viennes** *vyen*		tu veux que je **vienne** avec toi?
il/elle/on	**vienne** *vyen*		*too vuh kuh zhuh vyen a-vek twa?*
nous	**venions** *vuhn-yoñ*		
vous	**veniez** *vuhn-yay*		
ils/elles	**viennent** *vyen*		

Imperative		
(command)	**viens!** *vyañ!*	
	venons! *vuh-noñ!*	
	venez! *vuh-nay!*	

falloir (to be necessary)

Since **falloir** is an impersonal verb, only ever used with the pronoun **il**, it does not have all the normal parts.

Present	il	**faut** *eel foh*	you (*or* we) shouldn't arrive too late il ne **faut** pas arriver trop tard *eel nuh foh paz a-ree-vay troh tar*
Future	il	**faudra** *eel foh-dra*	you'll have to take your passport il **faudra** que tu prennes ton passeport *eel foh-dra kuh too pren toñ pass-por*
Past: perfect	il	**a fallu** *eel a fa-loo*	the police had to be called il **a fallu** appeler la police *eel a fa-loo ap-lay la po-leess*
Past: imperfect	il	**fallait** *eel fa-lay*	oh, that's kind! you shouldn't have! oh, c'est gentil! Il ne **fallait** pas! *oh, say zhoñ-tee! Eel nuh fa-lay pa*
Conditional	il	**faudrait** *eel foh-dray*	perhaps they should be warned il **faudrait** peut-être les prévenir *eel foo-dray puht-et-ruh lay pray-vuh-neer*
Subjunctive	il	**faille** *eel faee*	I do not think it is necessary to remain inside je ne pense pas qu'il **faille** rester à l'intérieur *zhuh nuh poñss pa keel faee res-tay a lañ-tay-ree-uhr*

Reflexive verbs

Reflexive verbs are those where the action is seen as happening to the person doing the same action. For example, in French you do not simply 'wash' or 'shave' but 'wash/shave yourself' (**se laver, se raser**). Reflexive verbs are more common in French than English.

Not all of them can be translated literally, just as you can't explain logically why in English you 'enjoy *yourself*'! This extra word **se** (and the English 'yourself') are known as reflexive pronouns. The reflexive pronouns (equivalent to 'myself', 'yourself' etc in English) are: **me, te, se, nous, vous, se** (**m', t', s', nous, vous, s'** before a vowel, most words beginning with **h**, and the French word **y**). The reflexive pronoun comes before the verb, except when you are telling someone to do something (the imperative or command). In the infinitive the pronoun **se** (oneself) is the one used.

The verb **être** is used to make the past tense of all reflexive verbs, not just the ones that normally take **être** rather than **avoir**: **je me suis lavé(e)** 'I washed' and **elles se sont amusées** 'they had fun'.

Some of the most common French reflexive verbs are listed here:

s'amuser *sa-moo-zay*	to enjoy yourself, to pass the time, to play
s'appeler *sap-lay*	to be called
s'arrêter *sa-ray-tay*	to stop
s'asseoir *sas-war*	to sit down
se coucher *suh koo-shay*	to go to bed, to lie down
se réveiller *suh ray-vay-yay*	to wake up
se lever *suh luh-vay*	to get/stand up, to rise
s'habiller *sab-ee-yay*	to get dressed
se laver *suh la-vay*	to wash, to have a wash

se baigner *suh ben-yay*	to bathe, have a bath
se dépêcher *suh day-pay-shay*	to hurry
se marier *suh mar-yay*	to get married
se passer *suh pa-say*	to happen
se promener *suh prom-nay*	to go for a walk
se rappeler *suh rap-play*	to remember
se trouver *suh troo-vay*	to be situated
s'entendre bien avec *soñ-toñ-druh byañ a-vek*	to get on well with
s'intéresser à *sañ-tay-ress-ay a*	to be interested in

what's happening?	**qu'est-ce qui se passe?** *kess kee suh pass?*
the sun rises at five o'clock	**le soleil se lève à cinq heures** *luh so-lay-ee suh lehv a sañk uhr*
I go to bed early	**je me couche tôt** *zhuh muh koosh toh*
sit down!	**asseyez-vous!** *a-say-ay voo!*
hurry up!	**dépêchez-vous!** *day-pesh-ay voo!*
don't get up!	**ne te lève pas!** *nuh tuh lehv pa!*
I had fun	**je me suis amusé(e)** *zuh muh sweez a-moo-zay*

need to know

In the past tense, all reflexive verbs count as être verbs.

se laver (to wash oneself)

Present			
	je	me lave *muh lav*	Béa is in the bathroom, she's washing
	tu	te laves *tuh lav*	Béa est dans la salle de bains, elle **se lave**
	il/elle/on	se lave *suh lav*	*bay-a ay doñ la sal duh bañ, el suh lav*
	nous	nous lavons *noo la-voñ*	
	vous	vous lavez *voo la-vay*	
	ils/elles	se lavent *suh lav*	

Future			
	je	me laverai *muh lav-ray*	we'll have breakfast and wash later
	tu	te laveras *tuh lav-ra*	on va prendre le petit déjeuner et on **se**
	il/elle/on	se lavera *suh lav-ra*	**lavera** plus tard
	nous	nous laverons *noo lav-roñ*	*oñ va proñ-druh luh puh-tee day-zhuh-nay ay oñ*
	vous	vous laverez *voo lav-ray*	*suh lav-ra ploo tar*
	ils/elles	se laveront *suh lav-roñ*	

Past: perfect			
	je	me suis lavé(e) *muh swee la-vay*	have you brushed (*literally* washed) your teeth?
	tu	t'es lavé(e) *tay la-vay*	tu **t'es lavé** les dents?
	il/elle/on	s'est lavé(e) *say la-vay*	*too tay lavay lay doñ?*
	nous	nous sommes lavé(e)s *noo som la-vay*	
	vous	vous êtes lavé(e)(s) *vooz et la-vay*	
	ils/elles	se sont lavé(e)s *suh soñ la-vay*	

Past: imperfect			
	je	me lavais *muh la-vay*	at that time they didn't have a bathroom,
	tu	te lavais *tuh la-vay*	they washed in the kitchen
	il/elle/on	se lavait *suh la-vay*	à l'époque, ils n'avaient pas de salle de bains,
	nous	nous lavions *noo lav-yoñ*	ils **se lavaient** dans la cuisine
	vous	vous laviez *voo lav-yay*	*a lay-pok, eel na-vay pa duh sal duh bañ, eel suh*
	ils/elles	se lavaient *suh la-vay*	*la-vay doñ la kwee-zeen*

Conditional			
	je	me laverais *muh lav-ray*	I wouldn't mind having a wash before having
	tu	te laverais *tuh lav-ray*	dinner
	il/elle/on	se laverait *suh lav-ray*	je **me laverais** bien avant de dîner
	nous	nous laverions *noo la-vuh-ryoñ*	*zhuh muh la-vuh-ray byañ a-voñ duh dee-nay*
	vous	vous laveriez *voo la-vuh-ryay*	
	ils/elles	se laveraient *suh lav-ray*	

Subjunctive			
	je	me lave *muh lav*	can I go into the bathroom before you wash?
	tu	te laves *tuh lav*	je peux aller dans la salle de bains avant que
	il/elle/on	se lave *suh lav*	vous **vous laviez**?
	nous	nous lavions *noo lav-yoñ*	*zhuh puh a-lay doñ la sal duh bañ a-voñ kuh voo*
	vous	vous laviez *voo lav-yay*	*voo lav-yay?*
	ils/elles	se lavent *suh lav*	

Imperative		
(command)	lave-toi! *lav-twa!*	
	lavons-nous! *la-voñ-noo!*	
	lavez-vous! *la-vay-voo!*	